"KAUTILYA'S ECONOMY"

Dr. Rakshit Madan Bagde

Assistant Professor & HOD Economics

Late. Mansaramji Padole College of Arts, Ganeshpur, Bhandara

M.A., M.PHIL., PH.D., NET

Year-2024

Foreword -

I am very happy to hand over to the readers the first edition of this book, **KAUTILYA'S ECONOMY.**

This book will be a useful text for students studying Bachelor of Art from various Universities of India. This book base on **NEP-2020** syllabus of **Indian Knowledge System (IKS) Course.**

I would like to express my sincere gratitude to all the authors whose books and opinions have been freely used in writing this reference book.

Since the subject is historical, it refers to many rare texts. Many distinguished congregations were involved in writing the book. I am thankful to Dr. Satyapriya Indurwade, Head of Economics Department, R.T.M. Nagpur University, Nagpur, Dr. Vijay Bansod, Mokhare College, Nagpur,. Also Thanks to Mrs. Samta Bagde and my son Master Smit & my all friends.

Dr. Rakshit Madan Bagde,

Assistant Professor,

Late. Mansaramji Padole Arts College, Ganeshpur Bhandara

ORCID iD - 0000-0002-7507-0244

SSRN - Author ID: 4770534

Vidwan-ID: 221858

RePEc Short-ID: pba1869

rakshitbagde@gmail.com

Indian Knowledge System (IKS) Course

Course Title: Kautilya's Economy

Course Code: BECO136IKS

KAUTILYA'S ECONOMY

Program: B.A. Semester - I (No. of Credits: 2)

Course Outcomes (COs): At the end of the course the student should be able to: 1. This course will enlighten the students about the ancient fundamentals about political and economic constituents, which will frame out a basic land of understanding the modern trends. This will help them to understand the upcoming needs in the area of policy making for states at national and international level.

2. This treatise deals with the science of Governance, so it projects out all the dimensions needed to be understood by students about the present socio-economic and political rules and regulations of the state.

CONTENTS:-

Unit-I: **Introduction of Kautilya's Arthashastra**

Content of his books Arthashastra', Concepts of Kautilya's Arthashastra, Origin, Influence, The welfare state, Good Governance, Foreign, trade, Taxation, Growth, Oriented Public Expenditure, Western perspective, Kautilya's Arthashastra, Problems in Kautilya's Arthashastra, Significance of Kautilya's Arthashastra, Arthashastra's Central Theme, Kautilya's categories of war, Kautilya's seven pillars, Ideology of Kautilya's, View of Kautilya's about Arthashastra, Principles of Arthashastra, Administrative ideas in Kautilya's Arthashastra, Saptanga Theory of Kautilya's Svami, Amaya, Janpada, Durga, Danda, Mitra

Unit-II: **Economic Thoughts of Kautilya's and its Contemporary Relevance Thought of Kautilya.**

A moral politics, Social Views, Contract theory of origin of state, Nature state, Welfare state, King, Kosh (Treasury): Danda, Durg, Janpad, Principle of Diplomacy, Strategies of Diplomacy, Mandala Theory & Kenneth Waltz, Machiavelli & Kautilya's

Economic Thought in Ancient India: Basic features, Economic ideas on Wealth & population, Land & Agriculture, Animal Husbandry, Labour, Wage & Social securities, Public finance & taxation, Pricing & price control, trade, Distribution, Economic functions of state.

CONTENTS

1. Kautilya's A moral politics.

2. Kautilya's Social Views.

3. Kautilya's Contract theory of origin of state.

4. Kautilya's Nature state.

5. Kautilya's Welfare state.

6. Kautilya's King.

7. Kautilya's Kosh. (Treasury)

8. Kautilya's Danda.

9. Kautilya's Durg.

10. Kautilya's Janpad.

11. Kautilya's Principle of Diplomacy.

12. Kautilya's Strategies of Diplomacy.

13. Kautilya's Mandala Theory & Kenneth Waltz.

14. Machiavelli & Kautilya's.

15. Economic Thought in Ancient India: Basic features.

16. Economic Thought in Ancient India - Economic ideas on Wealth & population.

17. Economic Thought in Ancient India -Land & Agriculture.

18. Economic Thought in Ancient India -Animal Husbandry.

19. Economic Thought in Ancient India –Labour.

20. Economic Thought in Ancient India -Wage & Social securities.

21. Economic Thought in Ancient India -Public finance & taxation.

22. Economic Thought in Ancient India -Pricing & price control.

23. Economic Thought in Ancient India –Trade.

24. Economic Thought in Ancient India –Distribution.

25. Economic Thought in Ancient India -Economic functions of state.

Unit-I: Introduction of Kautilya's Arthashastra.

1. Content of kautilya books Arthashastra.

Kautilya's Arthashastra is an ancient Indian treatise on statecraft, economic policy, and military strategy, attributed to Kautilya (also known as Chanakya or Vishnugupta). It is considered one of the most important texts on governance and administration in ancient India. The book is believed to have been written in the 4th century BCE, although some scholars suggest it could be earlier.

Here's an overview of the key content and themes of the Arthashastra:-

1. Statecraft and Administration.

I. The Role of the King: The king is the central figure in the Arthashastra. He is expected to be wise, just, and efficient, ruling with the welfare of his subjects in mind.

II. Council of Ministers: The text emphasizes the importance of a council of ministers to assist the king in governance. These ministers should be knowledgeable, loyal, and capable of giving sound advice.

III. Administrative Divisions: The kingdom is divided into various administrative units, each overseen by officials responsible for tax collection, law enforcement, and public welfare.

2. Economic Policy.

I. Revenue and Taxation: The Arthashastra provides detailed instructions on taxation, suggesting that taxes should be collected in a way that doesn't burden the populace but ensures a steady income for the state.

II. Agriculture: Agriculture is regarded as the backbone of the economy. The state is advised to promote agricultural productivity by providing incentives and ensuring the welfare of farmers.

III. Trade and Commerce: The text discusses the regulation of trade, including the establishment of markets, the role of the state in controlling prices, and the importance of foreign trade.

3. Law and Justice.

I. Legal System: The Arthashastra outlines a comprehensive legal system, including civil, criminal, and family law. It also details the procedures for trials, the role of judges, and the importance of justice in maintaining social order.

II. Punishments: The text prescribes various punishments for different crimes, emphasizing the need for justice to be swift and proportionate to the offense.

4. Military Strategy

I. Army Organization: The Arthashastra provides detailed guidelines on the organization of the military, including the recruitment, training, and deployment of troops.

II. War Tactics: The text discusses various strategies for warfare, including when to go to war, how to conduct sieges, and the importance of espionage.

III. Diplomacy: Kautilya emphasizes the use of diplomacy alongside military might. The text discusses various diplomatic strategies, including alliances, treaties, and espionage.

5. Espionage and Intelligence

I. Spies and Informants: The Arthashastra places significant importance on espionage as a tool for governance and military strategy. It describes how to recruit, train, and use spies to gather intelligence.

II. Surveillance: The text suggests that the state should keep a close watch on its subjects, especially those in positions of power, to prevent rebellion and corruption.

6. Ethics and Morality-

I. Pragmatism: The Arthashastra is known for its pragmatic approach to governance, sometimes advocating morally ambiguous actions if they serve the greater good of the state.

II. Dharmic Governance: While pragmatism is key, the text also acknowledges the importance of ruling in accordance with Dharma (moral law), balancing realpolitik with ethical considerations.

7. Miscellaneous Topics-

I. Infrastructure Development: The text provides guidelines on building roads, forts, and other public works.

II. Education and Training: It discusses the importance of education and training for both rulers and the general populace.

III. Health and Sanitation: The Arthashastra also addresses public health issues, including the importance of sanitation and the control of epidemics.

The Arthashastra is a comprehensive manual that covers nearly every aspect of governance, from politics and economics to warfare and law. Its influence extends beyond ancient India, offering timeless insights into the art of governance and the balance between power, ethics, and pragmatism.

2. Concepts of Kautilya's Arthashastra.

Kautilya's Arthashastra is a comprehensive treatise that presents a wide range of concepts related to governance, economics, military strategy, and statecraft. Here are some of the key concepts and principles that underpin the work:

1. Raj Mandala (Circle of States)

I. Geopolitical Theory: The concept of Raj Mandala describes the political and diplomatic relationships between neighbouring states. It is based on the idea that a king's immediate neighbours are his natural enemies, while states on the periphery are potential allies.

II. Alliances and Conflicts: Kautilya outlines strategies for forming alliances, managing conflicts, and expanding a kingdom's influence through diplomacy, war, and marriage alliances.

2. Saptanga Theory (The Seven Limbs of the State)

I. State as a Body: Kautilya views the state as a body composed of seven essential parts, which are:

1. Swamin (The King): The ruler, who must be wise and capable.

2. Amatya (The Ministers): Advisors and officials who assist in governance.

3. Janapada (The Population): The territory and the people who inhabit it.

4. Durga (The Fort): Fortifications and infrastructure, representing the state's defences.

5. Kosha (The Treasury): The economic resources and wealth of the state.

6. Danda (The Army): The military forces, crucial for protection and expansion.

7. Mitra (The Allies): External allies that support the state.

II. Interdependence: These elements are interdependent, and the prosperity of the state depends on the balance and effective functioning of all seven limbs.

3. Danda Neeti (The Policy of Punishment)

I. Law and Order: Danda Neeti refers to the use of force and punishment to maintain law and order in the state. Kautilya advocates for a strong legal system where justice is administered fairly but firmly.

II. Deterrence: The concept emphasizes the role of punishment as a deterrent against crime and disobedience. Kautilya believed that a ruler should not hesitate to use force to maintain stability.

4. Matsya Nyaya (Law of the Fish)

I. Anarchy and Power Struggles: Matsya Nyaya is the principle that in the absence of a strong authority, the stronger will naturally prey on the weaker—much like big fish eating small fish.

II. Justification for Strong Governance: This concept is used to justify the need for a powerful and centralized authority to prevent chaos and ensure the protection of the weak.

5. Dharma and Artha (Moral Duty and Material Gain)

I. Ethics vs. Pragmatism: While the Arthashastra is often seen as a pragmatic and sometimes ruthless guide to statecraft, Kautilya also acknowledges the importance of Dharma (moral duty) in governance.

II. Balancing Artha and Dharma: Kautilya advises rulers to pursue Artha (material prosperity) in a way that does not violate Dharma. The ideal ruler is one who balances the two, ensuring both the material and moral wellbeing of the state.

6. Sam, Dam, Dand, Bhed (Fourfold Policy)

I. Diplomatic Strategy: Kautilya outlines four methods of dealing with enemies:

1. Sam (Conciliation): Diplomacy and negotiation to resolve conflicts.

2. Dam (Gifts): Offering incentives or bribes to win over opponents.

3. Dand (Punishment): Use of force or coercion to subdue enemies.

4. Bhed (Division): Creating divisions among opponents to weaken them.

II.   Strategic Flexibility: The ruler should use these methods flexibly, depending on the situation, to achieve the desired outcome.

7. Shadgunya (Six Fold Policy)

I.   Foreign Policy: This concept refers to the six methods of foreign policy a king can adopt:

1. Sandhi (Peace Treaty): Forming alliances or making peace with enemies.

2. Vigraha (War): Engaging in warfare when necessary.

3. Asana (Neutrality): Maintaining a neutral stance in conflicts.

4. Yana (Military Campaign): Preparing for war or advancing against an enemy.

5. Samsraya (Seeking Shelter): Seeking protection from a stronger ally.

6. Dvaidhibhava (Dual Policy): Simultaneously pursuing two policies, such as making peace with one enemy while attacking another.

II.   Contextual DecisionMaking: The ruler must assess the situation carefully and choose the appropriate policy to protect and expand the kingdom.

8. Vyavahara (Civil and Criminal Law)

I.   Legal Framework: The Arthashastra provides detailed guidelines for the administration of justice, including civil and criminal law. It emphasizes the importance of a fair and efficient legal system to maintain social order.

II.   Punishments and Fines: Kautilya prescribes various punishments, fines, and other penalties for crimes, with the aim of deterring wrongdoing and maintaining harmony in society.

9. Arthashastra (The Science of Wealth)

I.   Economic Management: The term "Arthashastra" itself refers to the science of material wellbeing and economic management. Kautilya stresses the importance of a strong economy as the foundation of a powerful state.

II. Revenue Collection: The text discusses taxation, land revenue, trade, and other aspects of economic policy, advocating for efficient and just methods of resource management.

10. Rajaniti (The Art of Governance)

I. Principles of Governance: Rajaniti encompasses the principles and strategies of governance, including the selection of ministers, management of resources, and maintenance of law and order.

II. Role of the King: The king is expected to be a wise and just ruler, who governs with the welfare of his subjects in mind, balancing the pursuit of power with ethical considerations.

11. Raksha (Defence and Security)

I. National Defence: The Arthashastra provides extensive guidance on military strategy, the organization of the army, fortifications, and other aspects of defence. Kautilya emphasizes the need for a strong military to protect the state from external threats.

II. Espionage: Intelligence gathering through a network of spies is considered crucial for the security of the state. Kautilya outlines various methods of espionage to gather information on enemies and allies alike.

These concepts form the foundation of Kautilya's Arthashastra, offering a holistic view of governance that integrates ethics, economics, military strategy, and diplomacy. The text remains a seminal work in the study of ancient Indian political thought and continues to influence modern interpretations of statecraft and leadership.

3. Concepts of Kautilya's Arthashastra- Origin.

The concepts in Kautilya's Arthashastra are deeply rooted in ancient Indian philosophy, tradition, and the socio-political context of its time. The origins of these concepts can be traced to various sources, including earlier Vedic texts, Dharmashastras (religious law codes), and the practical realities of ancient Indian kingdoms.

1. Vedic and Dharmic Traditions

I.   Vedas: The Vedic texts, particularly the Rigveda, Yajurveda, and Atharvaveda, provide the earliest foundations for governance, social order, and morality in ancient India. The concepts of Dharma (righteousness) and Artha (material prosperity) are rooted in these texts.

II.   Dharmashastras: These are ancient Indian legal and ethical treatises that outline the duties of rulers, the administration of justice, and the maintenance of social order. The Manusmriti, one of the most important Dharmashastras, influenced Kautilya's ideas on law, justice, and the role of the king as a protector of Dharma.

2. Pragmatic Statecraft from Ancient Indian Kingdoms

I.   Mahajanapadas: The period of the Mahajanapadas (600–300 BCE), characterized by the emergence of large kingdoms and republics, provided a realworld backdrop for the development of concepts like Raj Mandala and the Saptanga theory. The political dynamics and interstate relations of this period influenced Kautilya's ideas on diplomacy, war, and alliances.

II.   Mauryan Empire: Kautilya is often associated with the rise of the Mauryan Empire, particularly the reign of Chandragupta Maurya. The practical challenges of consolidating power, managing a vast territory, and dealing with external threats likely informed the development of many of the Arthashastra's concepts.

3. Niti Shastra (Science of Politics) Tradition

I.   Niti (Policy and Morality): The Arthashastra is part of a broader tradition of Niti Shastra, which includes texts focused on political ethics, strategy, and governance. This tradition emphasizes the practical aspects of ruling, often advocating a realistic and sometimes ruthless approach to statecraft, which is evident in Kautilya's work.

II. Earlier Works: There were earlier works on politics and governance, such as the Arthashastras attributed to earlier sages like Brihaspati and Usanas. Kautilya's Arthashastra is considered a culmination and expansion of this earlier body of knowledge, incorporating and refining their ideas.

4. Realpolitik and Practical Governance

I. Matsya Nyaya: The concept of Matsya Nyaya, or the "Law of the Fish," reflects a pragmatic view of power dynamics in society, where the strong dominate the weak in the absence of a strong ruler. This idea may have originated from the observations of power struggles and conflicts in ancient Indian society, where the need for a central authority was evident.

II. Danda Neeti: The emphasis on Danda Neeti, or the policy of punishment, stems from the practical need to maintain order and discipline within the state. The concept likely evolved from the recognition that a ruler's ability to enforce laws and administer justice was crucial for the stability of the kingdom.

5. Influence of Earlier Thinkers

I. Brihaspati and Shukracharya: Kautilya's work is often compared to the teachings of earlier sages like Brihaspati (considered the teacher of the gods) and Shukracharya (the teacher of the demons). These figures are associated with earlier treatises on statecraft and economy, and Kautilya's Arthashastra is seen as building on and synthesizing their ideas.

II. Greco-Roman Influence: Some scholars suggest that Kautilya might have been influenced by the knowledge exchanges between India and the Hellenistic world, particularly after Alexander the Great's invasion of India. This interaction could have introduced new ideas on governance and military strategy that were incorporated into the Arthashastra.

6. Philosophical Underpinnings

I.   Lokayata (Materialism): The influence of Lokayata (also known as Carvaka), an ancient Indian school of materialist philosophy, is evident in the Arthashastra's emphasis on Artha (material wealth) as a central goal of human life and state policy. This pragmatic and sometimes cynical worldview aligns with the Arthashastra's focus on realpolitik.

II.   Sankhya and Yoga: Some concepts in the Arthashastra, such as the disciplined approach to governance and the strategic use of knowledge and information, may have been influenced by the Sankhya and Yoga schools of philosophy, which emphasize knowledge, analysis, and disciplined action.

7. Historical Context

I.   Post Vedic Society: The Arthashastra reflects the transition from a Vedic society, which was largely rural and tribal, to a more complex, urbanized, and politically fragmented society. This transition required new approaches to governance, economic management, and military strategy, which are addressed in the Arthashastra.

II.   Political Fragmentation: The political fragmentation and frequent conflicts between states during the time of the Mahajanapadas and the early Mauryan period likely influenced Kautilya's focus on diplomacy, warfare, and statecraft as essential tools for maintaining and expanding power.

8. Synthesis of Knowledge

I.   Compilation of Existing Knowledge: The Arthashastra is not just an original creation of Kautilya but also a compilation and synthesis of existing knowledge on governance, economics, and military strategy. Kautilya drew from various sources, including earlier texts, oral traditions, and his own experiences as a statesman, to create a comprehensive guide to ruling.

The concepts in the Arthashastra, therefore, have their origins in a combination of ancient Indian traditions, practical political experiences, and philosophical influences, all of which were synthesized by Kautilya to address the challenges of statecraft in his time.

4. Kautilya's Arthashastra- Influence.

Kautilya's Arthashastra has had a profound and lasting influence on various aspects of governance, political thought, and economic theory, both in ancient times and in the modern era. Here are some key areas where its influence can be observed:

1. Influence on Ancient Indian Governance

I.   Mauryan Empire: The Arthashastra is closely associated with the governance of the Mauryan Empire, particularly under Chandragupta Maurya. Kautilya, as the chief advisor to Chandragupta, is believed to have used the principles outlined in the Arthashastra to help establish and expand the empire, laying the foundations for one of the most powerful and welladministered states in ancient India.

II.   Statecraft and Administration: The text provided a detailed guide for rulers on how to organize their states, manage economies, and conduct diplomacy and warfare. Its principles were likely followed by subsequent Indian dynasties, influencing the way kingdoms were governed for centuries.

2. Impact on Political Thought

I.   Realpolitik: The Arthashastra is one of the earliest known works to advocate a pragmatic and sometimes ruthless approach to governance, emphasizing the importance of power and strategic thinking in statecraft. This has made it a seminal text in the tradition of realpolitik, influencing later thinkers and statesmen who prioritize practical considerations over idealistic ones.

II.   Comparisons with Machiavelli: Kautilya is often compared to Niccolò Machiavelli, the author of "The Prince," due to their similar approaches to power and governance. Both emphasized the importance of pragmatism, the use of deceit when necessary, and the centrality of the ruler in maintaining state power. This comparison has led to the Arthashastra being studied alongside other foundational works of political theory.

3. Economic and Military Strategy

I.   Foundations of Economics: The Arthashastra is considered one of the earliest works on economics and public finance. It discusses taxation, trade, agriculture, and resource management in great detail, influencing the development of economic thought in India and beyond. It laid the groundwork for later economic theories, especially in the context of state driven economies.

II.   Military Strategy and Defence: The Arthashastra's detailed guidelines on military organization, strategy, and intelligence have influenced military thought, particularly in the context of asymmetric warfare, the importance of espionage, and the use of alliances and diplomacy in military strategy.

4. Influence on Law and Justice

I.   Legal Tradition in India: The Arthashastra contributed to the development of the legal and judicial systems in ancient India. Its emphasis on justice, law enforcement, and the role of the state in maintaining order influenced the way law was practiced in various Indian kingdoms.

II.   Criminal and Civil Law: The text's detailed prescriptions for dealing with crime, corruption, and civil disputes have had a lasting impact on the formulation of laws and legal codes in subsequent Indian legal traditions.

5. Cultural and Philosophical Influence

I.   Dharma and Ethics: Despite its pragmatic approach, the Arthashastra also reflects the Indian cultural emphasis on Dharma (righteousness) and the ethical responsibilities of rulers. This balance between realpolitik and ethical governance has influenced Indian political philosophy, where rulers are expected to uphold both material prosperity (Artha) and moral order (Dharma).

II.   Integration of Philosophy and Statecraft: The Arthashastra's synthesis of various philosophical schools—such as the pragmatic Lokayata, the moralistic Dharmashastras, and the strategic Niti Shastra tradition—has influenced the way Indian thought integrates philosophy with practical governance.

6. Global Influence

I.   Modern Political Science: The Arthashastra is increasingly studied in the context of global political theory, particularly in the fields of international relations, diplomacy, and strategic studies. Its concepts, such as Raj Mandala (circle of states) and Shadgunya (six fold policy), are analyzed for their relevance in contemporary geopolitics.

II. Influence on Modern Indian Policy: Indian policymakers and strategists have revisited the Arthashastra in modern times, drawing on its principles for insights into statecraft, economic policy, and national security. The text's emphasis on selfreliance, strategic alliances, and economic management resonates with India's contemporary approach to governance and international relations.

7. Scholarly and Academic Impact

I. Historical and Textual Studies: The Arthashastra has been the subject of extensive scholarly study, particularly since its rediscovery in the early 20th century by the scholar R. Shamasastry. It has since been translated into various languages and analyzed for its historical significance and insights into ancient Indian society.

II. Comparative Political Theory: The Arthashastra is often included in comparative studies of political theory, alongside works like Machiavelli's "The Prince," Sun Tzu's "The Art of War," and Plato's "Republic." It provides a nonWestern perspective on governance that enriches the global understanding of political thought.

8. Literary and Cultural Legacy

I. Cultural References: The Arthashastra has influenced Indian literature and culture, with references to Kautilya and his principles appearing in various literary works, plays, and folk traditions. The figure of Kautilya has become emblematic of wisdom, cunning, and strategic brilliance in Indian culture.

II. Popular Media: In modern times, Kautilya and the Arthashastra have been referenced in popular media, including television series, films, and books, reflecting the enduring legacy of the text in Indian popular imagination.

9. Influence on Governance Models

I. Decentralization and Bureaucracy: The Arthashastra's emphasis on an efficient bureaucracy, clear administrative divisions, and the delegation of authority has influenced the development of governance models in India and other countries. The idea of a well-structured state with clearly defined roles for various officials is a legacy of the Arthashastra's administrative theories.

10. Ethical Leadership and Management

I. Leadership Studies: The Arthashastra's focus on the qualities of an ideal ruler—wisdom, decisiveness, ethical conduct, and strategic thinking—has influenced leadership studies, particularly in the context of ethical leadership and management practices.

The influence of Kautilya's Arthashastra extends far beyond its original context, impacting political, economic, and strategic thinking across centuries and continents. Its integration of pragmatic statecraft with ethical considerations continues to offer valuable insights into the complexities of governance and leadership.

5. Kautilya's Arthashastra-The welfare state.

Kautilya's Arthashastra is often cited as an early example of the concept of a welfare state, where the ruler is responsible for ensuring the wellbeing and prosperity of his subjects. While the Arthashastra is primarily known for its pragmatic approach to statecraft, it also places significant emphasis on the ruler's duty to promote the welfare of the people. This idea is woven throughout the text and reflects Kautilya's belief that a prosperous and stable state is built on the foundation of a content and wellcaredfor population.

1. Dharma and the King's Role

I. Ethical Governance: Kautilya emphasizes that the primary duty of the king is to uphold Dharma (righteousness and moral duty). This includes ensuring justice, protecting the weak, and promoting the general welfare of the people. The king's actions should be guided by the principle of Lokasangraha, which means the wellbeing of the entire society.

II. Moral Obligation: The Arthashastra portrays the king as a moral authority whose role is not just to rule but to ensure the prosperity, security, and happiness of his subjects. The king is seen as the "caretaker" of the people, with the state existing for the benefit of its citizens.

2. Economic Welfare

I. Promotion of Agriculture: The Arthashastra places great emphasis on the importance of agriculture as the backbone of the state's economy. The king is responsible for ensuring that land is properly irrigated, seeds are distributed, and farmers are supported in their work. Kautilya advises the king to provide assistance in times of drought or crop failure to prevent famine and social unrest.

II. State Involvement in Economy: The state is expected to play an active role in the economy by regulating trade, managing state-owned enterprises, and providing financial assistance to promote economic activities. This reflects a welfare oriented approach where the state takes direct responsibility for economic stability and growth.

3. Social Welfare and Public Works

I. Infrastructure Development: The Arthashastra advocates for the development of public infrastructure such as roads, water reservoirs, markets, and fortifications. These public works not only enhance the state's defence capabilities but also improve the quality of life for its citizens by facilitating trade, ensuring water supply, and providing security.

II. Healthcare and Public Health: The text mentions the need for public health measures, such as the establishment of hospitals and the provision of medical care, especially during times of epidemics. The state is expected to ensure that basic health services are available to the population.

4. Justice and Social Equity

I. Fair Legal System: Kautilya emphasizes the importance of a fair and efficient legal system that provides justice to all citizens, regardless of their social status. The king is advised to be impartial and to ensure that the courts are free from corruption. The protection of the weak, including women, children, and the poor, is a key aspect of this welfare approach.

II. Social Equity: The Arthashastra promotes the idea of social equity by advising the king to protect the interests of all classes of society, including the lower castes and marginalized groups. This includes measures to prevent exploitation, such as regulating wages, preventing unfair trade practices, and ensuring that workers receive fair treatment.

5. Disaster Relief and Social Security

I. Famine Relief and Food Security: The Arthashastra outlines specific measures for dealing with natural disasters such as famines. The king is advised to store surplus grain during times of plenty to distribute during famines. The state is also expected to provide loans to farmers and other citizens affected by such calamities.

II. Support for the Vulnerable: Kautilya's text includes provisions for providing support to vulnerable groups, such as the elderly, the disabled, and orphans. The state is expected to take responsibility for those who cannot fend for themselves, ensuring that they are not left destitute.

6. Education and Intellectual Welfare

I. Support for Education: The Arthashastra acknowledges the importance of education and intellectual development for the overall welfare of the state. The king is advised to patronize scholars, support educational institutions, and promote the study of various sciences and arts.

II. Encouragement of Cultural Activities: The state is also encouraged to support cultural activities, such as music, dance, and religious practices, which contribute to the overall wellbeing and happiness of the people.

7. Taxation and Economic Justice

I. Equitable Taxation: The Arthashastra advocates for a fair and just system of taxation, where taxes are levied based on the ability to pay. Kautilya advises the king to avoid excessive taxation, which could lead to poverty and social unrest. The goal of taxation is to ensure that the state has the resources to provide for the welfare of its citizens without imposing undue hardship.

II. Redistribution of Wealth: While Kautilya supports the accumulation of wealth by the state, he also emphasizes the need for redistribution through public spending on welfare programs, infrastructure, and relief measures. This reflects an early understanding of economic justice as a component of state welfare.

8. Environmental Welfare

I. Sustainable Resource Management: Kautilya's Arthashastra includes principles of sustainable resource management, advising the king to protect forests, wildlife, and natural resources. The welfare of the environment is seen as directly linked to the welfare of the people, as it ensures the availability of resources for future generations.

II. Conservation Efforts: The text also suggests that the king should establish protected areas and regulate the use of natural resources to prevent overexploitation and environmental degradation.

9. Welfare of Women and Children

I. Protection of Women: The Arthashastra advises the king to ensure the protection and welfare of women, particularly in matters of inheritance, marriage, and employment. The state is responsible for safeguarding women's rights and ensuring their safety and wellbeing.

II. Support for Children: Kautilya emphasizes the importance of providing for children, especially orphans and those from poor families. The state is expected to ensure that children receive proper care, education, and opportunities for growth.

10. Military and Security Welfare

I. Wellbeing of Soldiers: The welfare state concept in the Arthashastra extends to the military, where Kautilya advises the king to take care of the soldiers' needs, including fair pay, provisions for their families, and support in times of injury or death. A wellcaredfor army is seen as essential for the defence of the state and the protection of its people.

II. Security of Citizens: The text also emphasizes the importance of internal security and law enforcement to protect citizens from crime and unrest. The state's responsibility includes ensuring that people can live and work without fear of violence or exploitation.

11. Conclusion:

I. Benevolent Leadership: The overarching theme of the Arthashastra's welfare state is the idea of the king as a benevolent protector who governs not just with power but with compassion and foresight. The king is expected to act in the best interests of his subjects, ensuring that their material and moral needs are met.

II. Balance of Power and Welfare: Kautilya's vision of a welfare state is one where power is exercised with a sense of responsibility towards the people. The welfare of the state is directly linked to the welfare of its citizens, and a prosperous, stable, and secure state is the result of effective governance that prioritizes the common good.

In summary, Kautilya's Arthashastra presents a comprehensive vision of a welfare state where the ruler is tasked with ensuring the wellbeing of his subjects through ethical governance, economic management, social equity, and the provision of public goods. This vision remains relevant as a historical example of how early political thought addressed the responsibilities of the state towards its people.

6. Kautilya's Arthashastra-Good Governance.

Kautilya's Arthashastra provides one of the earliest and most comprehensive treatises on the principles of good governance. Kautilya (also known as Chanakya or Vishnugupta) emphasizes that a well governed state is essential for the prosperity and security of the kingdom. The text outlines various elements that contribute to good governance, including the qualities of a ruler, the structure of administration, justice, and ethical conduct.

1. Qualities of the Ruler

I. Wisdom and Knowledge: Kautilya emphasizes that a good ruler must be knowledgeable and wise. The king should be wellversed in various sciences, including economics, law, politics, and military strategy. A wellinformed ruler is better equipped to make decisions that benefit the state and its people.

II. Moral Integrity: The ruler must possess moral integrity and adhere to Dharma (righteousness). Kautilya stresses that a ruler should lead by example, maintaining personal discipline and ethical conduct. The king's behaviour sets the standard for the rest of the administration and the citizens.

III. Decisiveness and Courage: A good ruler should be decisive and courageous, capable of making difficult decisions in times of crisis. The ability to act swiftly and confidently is crucial for maintaining order and stability in the state.

IV. Compassion and Justice: While being firm, the ruler must also be compassionate and just. Kautilya advises that a ruler should be fair in dispensing justice and considerate of the welfare of all subjects, particularly the poor and vulnerable.

2. Effective Administration

I. Centralized Authority: The Arthashastra advocates for a centralized form of government where the king holds ultimate authority but delegates responsibilities to a well-structured bureaucracy. This ensures that decisions are made efficiently and that there is clear accountability within the administration.

II. Efficient Bureaucracy: Kautilya outlines a detailed administrative structure, with ministers and officials responsible for various aspects of governance, such as finance, defence, and law enforcement. These officials are expected to be competent, loyal, and dedicated to their duties.

III. Regular Audits and Inspections: To ensure good governance, Kautilya recommends regular audits and inspections of various departments. This helps prevent corruption, inefficiency, and abuse of power. Officials are held accountable for their actions, and those found guilty of misconduct are punished.

IV. MeritBased Appointments: The Arthashastra advocates for the appointment of officials based on merit rather than heredity or favoritism. Competence, experience, and loyalty are the key criteria for selecting administrators, which ensures that the most capable individuals are in positions of power.

3. Justice and Legal System

I. Impartial Justice: A key component of good governance, according to Kautilya, is an impartial and fair legal system. The king is expected to be the highest authority in judicial matters, ensuring that justice is administered without bias or corruption.

II. Protection of the Weak: The legal system should protect the rights of the weak, including women, children, and the poor. Kautilya emphasizes the importance of laws that safeguard these groups from exploitation and injustice.

III. Punishment and Rehabilitation: While the Arthashastra advocates for strict enforcement of laws and appropriate punishment for crimes, it also recognizes the importance of rehabilitation. The goal of punishment is not only to deter crime but also to reform offenders and reintegrate them into society.

4. Economic Management

I. Sustainable Economic Policies: Kautilya stresses the importance of economic prosperity for the state's stability. The ruler should promote agriculture, trade, and industry, ensuring that resources are managed sustainably and that the economy is diversified.

II. Fair Taxation: Good governance requires a fair and efficient taxation system. Kautilya advises that taxes should be levied according to the ability to pay and should not be so burdensome as to impoverish the people. The revenue generated from taxes should be used to fund public goods and services, such as infrastructure, education, and welfare.

III. Public Works: Investment in public works, such as roads, irrigation, and fortifications, is seen as a key responsibility of the state. These projects not only improve the quality of life for citizens but also enhance the state's economic and military capabilities.

5. Military and Security

I. Strong Defence: Kautilya considers a strong military essential for the security of the state. Good governance includes maintaining a well-trained and well-equipped army that can defend the kingdom from external threats and maintain internal order.

II. Intelligence and Espionage: The Arthashastra places significant emphasis on the role of intelligence and espionage in governance. A good ruler should have a well-developed network of spies to gather information about potential threats, both internal and external. This allows the state to preemptively address issues before they escalate.

III. Internal Security: In addition to defending against external threats, the ruler must ensure internal security by maintaining law and order. This includes preventing and suppressing rebellions, riots, and other forms of unrest.

6. Diplomacy and Foreign Relations

I. Strategic Alliances: Kautilya advises rulers to engage in diplomacy and form strategic alliances to strengthen their position. Good governance includes the ability to negotiate treaties, form alliances, and manage relationships with neighbouring states to maintain peace and stability.

II. Realpolitik: The Arthashastra is known for its pragmatic approach to diplomacy. Kautilya encourages rulers to act in the best interests of their state, using any means necessary, including deception, if it serves the greater good. This approach to foreign policy is centred on the principle of self-interest and the pursuit of power.

7. Ethics and Morality in Governance

I. Balance of Dharma and Artha: Kautilya's vision of good governance involves balancing Dharma (moral duty) and Artha (material wealth). While the pursuit of wealth and power is important, it should not come at the expense of ethical conduct. The ruler must ensure that economic and political strategies align with the principles of righteousness.

II. Ethical Leadership: The Arthashastra emphasizes the importance of ethical leadership. A ruler who acts with integrity, fairness, and justice earns the respect and loyalty of the people, which in turn contributes to the stability and prosperity of the state.

8. Public Welfare

I. Welfare of Citizens: Good governance, according to Kautilya, requires a focus on the welfare of the citizens. The state should ensure that the basic needs of the people, such as food, shelter, and security, are met. Public health, education, and infrastructure are also important components of a welfare oriented state.

II. Disaster Relief: The Arthashastra outlines the responsibilities of the state in times of disaster, such as famines or floods. The ruler is expected to provide relief and support to the affected population, ensuring that no one is left destitute.

9. Accountability and Transparency

I. Transparency in Governance: Kautilya advocates for transparency in governance, where the ruler and officials are open about their actions and decisions. This builds trust between the state and the people, reducing the potential for corruption and abuse of power.

II. Accountability of Officials: The Arthashastra emphasizes the importance of holding officials accountable for their actions. Regular audits, inspections, and evaluations are necessary to ensure that officials perform their duties effectively and ethically.

10. Sustainability and LongTerm Planning

I. LongTerm Vision: Good governance, according to Kautilya, involves longterm planning and sustainability. The ruler should not only focus on immediate gains but also consider the longterm impact of policies on the state's prosperity and stability.

II. Succession Planning: Kautilya also advises rulers to plan for succession to ensure a smooth transition of power. This is important for maintaining continuity in governance and preventing power struggles that could destabilize the state.

11. Conclusion: The Ideal State

I. The Role of the King: In Kautilya's vision of good governance, the king is central to the wellbeing of the state. A ruler who governs with wisdom, fairness, and a focus on the welfare of the people creates a stable and prosperous state. The Arthashastra presents a model of governance where power is exercised with responsibility, and the ruler's success is measured by the prosperity and contentment of the subjects.

II. Saptanga Theory: Kautilya's Saptanga (Seven Limbs) theory also encapsulates his idea of good governance. This theory outlines the seven essential elements of a state: the king, the ministers, the territory, the fortified city, the treasury, the army, and the allies. A wellfunctioning state depends on the proper management and integration of these elements.

Kautilya's Arthashastra provides a timeless framework for good governance, blending pragmatism with ethical considerations and emphasizing the ruler's duty to ensure the prosperity and security of the state. Its principles remain relevant in discussions of governance, leadership, and statecraft even today.

7. Kautilya's Arthashastra-Foreign.

Kautilya's Arthashastra offers a detailed and pragmatic approach to foreign policy, emphasizing the importance of diplomacy, strategic alliances, and realpolitik in maintaining and expanding the power of the state. Kautilya's approach to foreign relations is characterized by a keen understanding of human nature, the dynamics of power, and the necessity of flexibility in achieving state objectives. The principles outlined in the Arthashastra continue to influence modern diplomatic strategies and theories of international relations.

1. The Mandala Theory of Foreign Relations

I.   Concept of Mandala: Kautilya's Mandala theory is a framework for understanding the geopolitical environment in which a state operates. According to this theory, states are positioned in a circle (mandala) of concentric rings, with the central state (the vijigishu, or wouldbe conqueror) surrounded by other states classified as enemies (ari), allies (mitra), neutral states (madhyama), and those that can be exploited (udasina).

II. Relationship Dynamics: The Arthashastra advises the ruler to assess the relationships between these states carefully. The theory suggests that neighbouring states are natural enemies, while states on the other side of the enemy are potential allies. This understanding helps the ruler form alliances, neutralize threats, and strategically expand influence.

2. SixFold Policy (Shadgunya)

I.   Six Strategies: Kautilya outlines six primary strategies that a ruler can adopt in foreign policy:

1. Peace (Sandhi): Making peace with a stronger power or when the state needs time to strengthen itself.

2. War (Vigraha): Engaging in war when the state is strong and likely to achieve victory.

3. Neutrality (Asana): Remaining neutral when it is not advantageous to engage in either peace or war.

4. Marching (Yana): Preparing for war or showing strength by mobilizing the army.

5. Alliance (Samsraya): Forming alliances with other states to counter a common threat.

6. Double Policy (Dvaidhibhava): Simultaneously pursuing peace with one state while waging war with another.

II.   Contextual Flexibility: The Arthashastra emphasizes that the choice of strategy should be based on a careful analysis of the situation, considering the relative strengths and weaknesses of the states involved, as well as the longterm interests of the kingdom.

3. Realpolitik and Pragmatism

I.   Pragmatic Approach: Kautilya advocates for a realistic and pragmatic approach to foreign policy, where the primary goal is the protection and expansion of the state's power. Ethical considerations, while important, are secondary to the practical needs of the state. The ruler is encouraged to use any means necessary—diplomacy, deceit, or force—to achieve the desired outcomes.

II.   Deception and Diplomacy: The Arthashastra suggests that deception can be a legitimate tool in diplomacy. For instance, the ruler might feign friendship to buy time or weaken an enemy before striking. Kautilya's famous maxim, "My enemy's enemy is my friend," reflects this pragmatic approach to alliances and enmity.

4. Alliances and Treaties

I.   Strategic Alliances: Kautilya advises forming alliances based on mutual benefit and strategic necessity. These alliances can be temporary or long term, depending on the changing dynamics of power. The ruler should always seek to gain more from an alliance than the ally, ensuring that the state's interests are prioritized.

II.   Treaty Negotiations: In treaty negotiations, Kautilya emphasizes the importance of maintaining a position of strength. He advises that treaties should be designed to enhance the state's security and economic interests. If necessary, the ruler should not hesitate to break a treaty if it no longer serves the state's interests or if the ally becomes a potential threat.

5. Espionage and Intelligence Gathering

I. Role of Spies: Espionage is a crucial element of Kautilya's foreign policy. The Arthashastra provides detailed instructions on the use of spies to gather intelligence on foreign states, their rulers, military capabilities, and internal conditions. This intelligence is vital for making informed decisions in diplomacy and warfare.

II. CounterIntelligence: In addition to gathering intelligence, Kautilya also emphasizes the importance of counterintelligence to protect the state from enemy spies. The ruler should be aware of potential threats from within and take measures to neutralize them.

6. Power Dynamics and Balance of Power

I. Balance of Power: Kautilya's foreign policy is deeply rooted in the concept of maintaining a balance of power. The ruler should aim to prevent any single state from becoming too powerful and threatening the security of the kingdom. This can be achieved by forming alliances, supporting weaker states, or directly intervening when a neighbouring state becomes too dominant.

II. Exploiting Rivalries: The Arthashastra advises the ruler to exploit rivalries between neighbouring states to maintain this balance. By supporting one state against another or encouraging conflict between rivals, the ruler can weaken potential threats and strengthen their own position.

7. Use of Force and War

I. Justification for War: While Kautilya prefers diplomacy, he recognizes that war is sometimes necessary. The Arthashastra outlines conditions under which war is justified, such as when the state's security is threatened or when there is an opportunity for territorial expansion that will strengthen the state.

II. Types of War: Kautilya classifies wars into three categories:

1. Open War: A direct and declared conflict between states.

2. Covert War: Involving the use of espionage, sabotage, and assassination to weaken the enemy from within.

3. Silent War: A strategic war of attrition where the ruler weakens the enemy through economic sanctions, blockades, or by fomenting internal dissent.

4. War Ethics: Despite his pragmatic approach, Kautilya acknowledges the ethical aspects of war, advising rulers to minimize unnecessary suffering and avoid harming civilians whenever possible.

8. Diplomatic Envoys and Negotiation

I. Role of Diplomats: Diplomats play a crucial role in Kautilya's foreign policy. The Arthashastra advises rulers to appoint skilled and trustworthy envoys who can represent the state's interests effectively in foreign courts. These diplomats should be wellversed in rhetoric, negotiation tactics, and the political landscape of the states they are dealing with.

II. Negotiation Tactics: Kautilya emphasizes the importance of negotiation in resolving conflicts and securing favorable treaties. The Arthashastra provides guidance on various negotiation tactics, including persuasion, intimidation, and compromise, depending on the situation and the relative power of the states involved.

9. Economic Diplomacy

I. Trade Relations: Kautilya recognizes the importance of economic strength in foreign policy. The Arthashastra advises rulers to use trade relations as a tool of diplomacy. By controlling trade routes, imposing tariffs, or offering trade concessions, the ruler can influence the policies of other states and strengthen the kingdom's economic position.

II. Resource Management: The text also highlights the importance of securing and managing resources, such as minerals, water, and agricultural products, which are vital for both domestic prosperity and diplomatic leverage.

10. Long Term Strategic Planning

I. Vision for Expansion: Kautilya's foreign policy is not just about immediate gains but also long term strategic planning. The Arthashastra advises rulers to think several steps ahead, considering the longterm implications of alliances, wars, and diplomatic actions. The ultimate goal is to expand the state's influence and ensure its dominance in the region.

II. Succession and Continuity: Kautilya also emphasizes the importance of planning for succession and ensuring continuity in foreign policy. A stable succession plan ensures that the state's long term strategic goals are not disrupted by internal power struggles.

11. Ethical Considerations and State Interests

I.   Balancing Ethics and Pragmatism: While Kautilya is often viewed as a proponent of realpolitik, he does not completely dismiss ethical considerations. The Arthashastra advises rulers to balance ethical conduct with pragmatic decisionmaking. For instance, while deceit may be used in diplomacy, it should not lead to long term mistrust or damage the ruler's reputation.

II.   State Interests as Paramount: Ultimately, the primary focus of Kautilya's foreign policy is the interest of the state. Ethical considerations, while important, are secondary to the survival and prosperity of the kingdom. The ruler must always prioritize the state's security, power, and wealth in foreign relations.

12. Conclusion: A Blueprint for Diplomatic Strategy

I.   Comprehensive Foreign Policy: Kautilya's Arthashastra offers a comprehensive blueprint for foreign policy that is both flexible and pragmatic. It combines a deep understanding of human nature, power dynamics, and geopolitical realities with a focus on the state's long term interests.

II.   Legacy and Modern Relevance: The principles outlined in the Arthashastra continue to be relevant in modern diplomacy and international relations. Kautilya's emphasis on strategic alliances, the balance of power, and the pragmatic use of force and diplomacy are concepts that resonate with contemporary foreign policy strategies.

In essence, Kautilya's Arthashastra provides a timeless guide to foreign policy, advocating a blend of realpolitik and ethical considerations, all aimed at securing the state's power, stability, and prosperity in a complex and competitive international environment.

8. Kautilya's Arthashastra-Trade.

Kautilya's Arthashastra places significant emphasis on trade as a crucial aspect of the state's economy and overall prosperity. Kautilya (also known as Chanakya) views trade not just as a means of economic growth but as a vital tool for statecraft, diplomacy, and security. The Arthashastra outlines detailed guidelines for managing trade, including the regulation of markets, taxation, trade routes, and the role of the state in facilitating and controlling economic activities.

1. Importance of Trade in the State Economy

I.   Economic Prosperity: Kautilya recognizes trade as a key driver of economic prosperity. The Arthashastra emphasizes that a strong trade network enhances the wealth of the state, which in turn supports its military and administrative functions. A prosperous economy leads to a stable and powerful state.

II.   Resource Management: The text underscores the importance of trade in ensuring the efficient management of resources. Kautilya advises that the state should facilitate the import of essential goods that are not available locally and encourage the export of surplus products. This helps maintain a balanced economy and prevents scarcity.

2. State Control and Regulation of Trade

I.   Regulation of Markets: The Arthashastra advocates for state control over markets to prevent exploitation and ensure fair trade practices. The state appoints a superintendent of trade (Panyadhyaksha) responsible for overseeing market activities, regulating prices, and ensuring that goods meet quality standards.

II.   Price Control: To prevent inflation and protect consumers, Kautilya recommends setting maximum prices for essential goods. The state can intervene in the market to stabilize prices, especially during times of crisis, such as famines or natural disasters.

III.   Monopolies and State Enterprises: Kautilya allows for state run monopolies in certain critical sectors, such as mining, salt production, and forest products. These state enterprises ensure a steady revenue stream for the state and control over essential resources.

3. Taxation and Revenue from Trade

I. Fair Taxation: The Arthashastra provides a framework for the taxation of trade. Kautilya advises that taxes on trade should be fair and not excessively burdensome to traders, as this could discourage commerce. The state should collect taxes from both domestic and foreign traders based on the value of goods traded.

II. Customs Duties: The text outlines the collection of customs duties on goods entering and leaving the state. Kautilya suggests that these duties should be reasonable and structured to encourage trade while providing revenue for the state. Smuggling and tax evasion are strictly prohibited and punished to protect state revenues.

III. Licenses and Permits: Traders are required to obtain licenses or permits from the state to operate in markets or transport goods. The state uses this system to monitor and regulate trade activities, ensuring compliance with laws and collecting appropriate fees.

4. Trade Routes and Infrastructure

I. Maintenance of Trade Routes: Kautilya emphasizes the importance of maintaining and securing trade routes, both within the state and with neighbouring regions. Well-maintained roads, ports, and waterways facilitate smooth trade and reduce transportation costs.

II. Protection of Traders: The Arthashastra advises the state to ensure the safety of traders and caravans. This includes protecting them from bandits, pirates, and other threats. Providing security for traders encourages commerce and strengthens the state's economy.

III. Control of Strategic Locations: Kautilya recognizes the strategic importance of controlling key trade routes and locations, such as ports, border posts, and major crossroads. By controlling these areas, the state can regulate trade flows, collect taxes, and exert influence over neighbouring regions.

5. Foreign Trade and Diplomacy

I. Encouraging Foreign Trade: The Arthashastra encourages the state to engage in foreign trade to acquire goods that are not available domestically and to expand the state's influence. Kautilya advises the ruler to establish and maintain good relations with neighbouring states and distant regions to facilitate trade.

II. Trade as Diplomacy: Kautilya views trade as a tool of diplomacy. Trade agreements and partnerships can be used to strengthen alliances, create dependencies, and extend the state's influence. By controlling the supply of certain goods, the state can gain leverage over other states.

III. Regulation of Foreign Traders: Foreign traders are subject to state regulations and taxes. Kautilya advises that foreign traders be treated fairly to encourage their business, but they should also be carefully monitored to prevent espionage or subversive activities.

6. Role of the State in Promoting Trade

I. Promotion of Industry: The Arthashastra advises the state to promote industries that produce goods for both domestic consumption and export. The state can offer incentives, such as tax breaks or subsidies, to encourage the growth of key industries.

II. Investment in Public Works: Kautilya emphasizes the importance of state investment in infrastructure, such as roads, warehouses, and markets, to support trade. These public works projects not only facilitate commerce but also create jobs and stimulate economic growth.

III. Crisis Management: The state should be prepared to intervene in the economy during times of crisis, such as crop failures or trade disruptions. Kautilya advises the state to stockpile essential goods and provide relief to prevent economic collapse.

IV. 7. Ethics and Trade Practices

V. Fair Trade Practices: Kautilya advocates for ethical trade practices. The Arthashastra advises against fraudulent activities, such as adulteration of goods, deceptive pricing, and hoarding. Traders who engage in unethical practices should be punished to maintain market integrity.

VI. Protection of Consumers: The state has a responsibility to protect consumers from exploitation. Kautilya advises the establishment of mechanisms for consumers to report grievances and seek redress. Ensuring consumer protection fosters trust in the market and promotes stable trade relations.

8. Trade and Social Welfare

I.   Employment and Livelihoods: Trade and commerce are seen as vital for providing employment and supporting livelihoods. Kautilya emphasizes the role of the state in creating a favourable environment for trade, which in turn contributes to social stability and reduces poverty.

II.   Public Welfare Projects: Revenue generated from trade is to be used by the state to fund public welfare projects, such as education, healthcare, and infrastructure development. This ensures that the benefits of trade are distributed widely and contribute to the overall wellbeing of the population.

9. Merchant Guilds and Trade Organizations

I.   Role of Guilds: The Arthashastra acknowledges the role of merchant guilds and trade organizations in regulating trade practices, setting standards, and representing the interests of traders. These guilds are important for maintaining order in the markets and ensuring that trade operates smoothly.

II.   State and Guild Relations: Kautilya advises the state to maintain good relations with merchant guilds, recognizing their influence and importance in the economy. However, the state should also ensure that these organizations do not become too powerful or corrupt.

10. Conclusion: Trade as a Pillar of State Power

I.   Foundation of Prosperity: In Kautilya's vision, trade is a foundational pillar of state power. A well-regulated and prosperous trade network strengthens the state economically, politically, and militarily.

II.   Legacy in Economic Thought: The principles outlined in the Arthashastra regarding trade continue to influence economic thought and policy. Kautilya's emphasis on state control, fair taxation, infrastructure development, and ethical practices remains relevant in discussions of trade and commerce today.

In summary, Kautilya's Arthashastra presents trade as a vital aspect of governance, with the state playing a central role in regulating, promoting, and benefiting from commercial activities. The text offers a comprehensive approach to trade, integrating economic prosperity with broader goals of state security, diplomacy, and social welfare.

9. Kautilya's Arthashastra-Taxation.

Kautilya's Arthashastra provides a detailed and systematic approach to taxation, viewing it as a critical component of statecraft. Taxation in the Arthashastra is designed to support the state's administrative, military, and welfare functions while ensuring economic stability and fairness. Kautilya's principles of taxation emphasize efficiency, justice, and the maximization of state revenue without overburdening the population.

1. Purpose of Taxation

I.   Revenue for the State: The primary purpose of taxation in the Arthashastra is to generate revenue for the state. This revenue is essential for maintaining the administration, funding the military, and implementing public welfare programs.

II.   Economic Stability: Kautilya views taxation as a tool for maintaining economic stability. By carefully adjusting tax rates and policies, the state can influence economic activities, control inflation, and prevent the concentration of wealth.

III.   Social Welfare: A portion of the revenue generated through taxation is allocated to public welfare projects, such as infrastructure development, healthcare, and education. This ensures that the benefits of taxation are distributed across society.

2. Principles of Taxation

I.   Fairness and Equity: Kautilya emphasizes that taxes should be fair and equitable. The burden of taxation should be distributed according to the ability to pay, with wealthier individuals and those with higher incomes contributing more. This principle ensures that the tax system does not disproportionately affect the poor.

II.   Avoiding Over Taxation: The Arthashastra warns against excessive taxation, which could lead to public discontent, economic stagnation, and even rebellion. Kautilya advises that tax rates should be set at a level that is sustainable and does not discourage productivity or trade.

III.   Regular and Predictable Taxes: Taxes should be regular and predictable, allowing individuals and businesses to plan accordingly. Sudden or arbitrary changes in taxation can lead to economic instability and loss of trust in the government.

3. Types of Taxes

I. Land Revenue (Bhaga): One of the most important taxes in the Arthashastra is the land revenue tax, known as "Bhaga." This tax is typically a share of the agricultural produce, usually set at onesixth (or more) of the produce. The state collects this tax from farmers and landowners based on the fertility of the land and the type of crops grown.

II. Customs Duties (Shulka): Taxes on goods imported and exported through the state's borders are known as customs duties. These taxes are an essential source of revenue and also serve to regulate trade. The rates of customs duties can vary depending on the type of goods and their origin.

III. Tolls (Sulka): Tolls are collected at various checkpoints along trade routes, bridges, and ports. These are fees charged for the use of infrastructure and are a way for the state to recoup the costs of maintaining these facilities.

IV. Commercial Taxes (Kara): Traders and merchants are subject to taxes on their commercial activities. These taxes are based on the value of goods sold, the volume of trade, and the profits made. The Arthashastra includes detailed guidelines on the assessment and collection of these taxes.

V. Excise Duties: Taxes are also levied on the production and sale of certain goods, particularly luxury items like alcohol, textiles, and perfumes. These excise duties help generate revenue from nonessential goods and can be adjusted to reflect changes in consumption patterns.

VI. Tributes and Concessions: Vassal states, conquered territories, and allied kingdoms may be required to pay tributes or special taxes. These payments can be in the form of goods, money, or services and are often negotiated as part of treaties or agreements.

4. Tax Collection and Administration

I. Role of Tax Collectors: The Arthashastra outlines the role of tax collectors, who are responsible for assessing, collecting, and remitting taxes to the state treasury. These officials must be honest, efficient, and well-trained to ensure that taxes are collected fairly and accurately.

II. Prevention of Corruption: Kautilya is aware of the potential for corruption among tax collectors. The Arthashastra includes strict penalties for officials who engage in corruption, embezzlement, or other forms of misconduct. Regular audits and inspections are recommended to ensure transparency and accountability.

III. Record Keeping: Detailed records of taxes collected, payments made, and revenues generated are essential for effective tax administration. The Arthashastra advises maintaining accurate and up-to-date records to monitor the efficiency of the tax system and prevent fraud.

5. Incentives and Relief Measures

I. Tax Incentives: The Arthashastra suggests that the state can offer tax incentives to encourage certain economic activities, such as agriculture, trade, or manufacturing. These incentives can take the form of reduced tax rates, tax holidays, or exemptions for specific industries.

II. Relief During Hardship: In times of hardship, such as droughts, floods, or other natural disasters, the state should provide tax relief to affected populations. This might include reducing or suspending taxes temporarily to allow people to recover and maintain economic stability.

III. Support for the Poor: Kautilya recognizes the need to support the poor and marginalized sections of society. The Arthashastra advises that certain groups, such as widows, orphans, and the disabled, should be exempt from certain taxes or provided with financial assistance from the state.

6. Use of Tax Revenue

I. Public Welfare: A significant portion of tax revenue should be allocated to public welfare projects. This includes the construction of roads, bridges, and public buildings; the provision of healthcare and education; and the maintenance of law and order.

II. Military and Defence: Funding the military is a crucial use of tax revenue. The Arthashastra emphasizes the need for a strong and well-equipped military to protect the state from external threats and maintain internal security.

III. Administrative Expenses: Tax revenue also covers the costs of running the government, including the salaries of officials, the maintenance of government buildings, and other administrative expenses.

IV.   Emergency Funds: Kautilya advises that the state should set aside a portion of tax revenue as a reserve for emergencies. This fund can be used in times of war, natural disasters, or other unforeseen events that require immediate financial resources.

7. Ethics and Justice in Taxation

I.   Ethical Considerations: Kautilya stresses the importance of ethics in taxation. The state should not exploit its citizens through unjust or oppressive taxes. The ruler has a moral duty to ensure that taxation is conducted fairly and that the revenue is used for the benefit of the people.

II.   Justice in Disputes: The Arthashastra provides guidelines for resolving tax disputes between the state and its citizens. Disputes should be settled in a just and transparent manner, with provisions for appeals and reviews to ensure fairness.

8. Adaptability and Flexibility

I.   Adjusting Tax Policies: Kautilya recognizes that tax policies must be adaptable to changing economic conditions. The Arthashastra advises the ruler to regularly review and adjust tax rates, exemptions, and collection methods to reflect the current state of the economy.

II.   Responding to Economic Changes: The state should be responsive to economic changes, such as shifts in trade patterns, technological advancements, or changes in population. Tax policies should be flexible enough to accommodate these changes and ensure continued revenue generation.

9. Impact on Economic Growth

I.   Promoting Economic Growth: Kautilya's taxation policies are designed to promote economic growth by encouraging productivity, trade, and investment. By keeping taxes fair and reasonable, the state can foster an environment conducive to economic development.

II.   Preventing Economic Decline: The Arthashastra warns against tax policies that could lead to economic decline, such as excessive taxation or arbitrary tax increases. These policies can reduce incentives for production and trade, leading to economic stagnation and a decrease in state revenue.

10. Conclusion: Taxation as a Tool of Governance

I. Integral to Statecraft: In Kautilya's vision, taxation is not merely a means of raising revenue but a fundamental tool of governance. Effective taxation supports the state's stability, security, and prosperity.

II. Legacy and Modern Relevance: The principles of taxation outlined in the Arthashastra continue to influence modern economic and fiscal policies. Kautilya's emphasis on fairness, efficiency, and the ethical use of tax revenue remains relevant in contemporary discussions on taxation and governance.

In summary, Kautilya's Arthashastra provides a comprehensive framework for taxation, highlighting its importance in statecraft and governance. Through fair and efficient tax policies, the state can ensure its financial health, support public welfare, and maintain social and economic stability.

10. Kautilya's Arthashastra-Growth.

Kautilya's Arthashastra emphasizes growth as a fundamental objective of governance, with a focus on economic, social, and political development. Kautilya (also known as Chanakya) advocates for a well-rounded approach to growth, integrating economic prosperity, military strength, social welfare, and efficient governance. His vision of growth is deeply tied to the stability and security of the state, with the ultimate goal of creating a powerful and prosperous kingdom.

1. Economic Growth

I. Agriculture as the Foundation: Kautilya views agriculture as the backbone of the economy and the primary source of wealth. He advocates for state support in improving agricultural practices, ensuring adequate irrigation, and providing farmers with necessary resources. A thriving agricultural sector is seen as essential for food security and the overall prosperity of the state.

II. Promotion of Trade and Commerce: The Arthashastra places significant emphasis on trade and commerce as drivers of economic growth. Kautilya encourages the state to develop infrastructure, such as roads, ports, and markets, to facilitate trade. He also supports the regulation of trade to ensure fair practices and prevent exploitation.

III. Industry and Manufacturing: Kautilya recognizes the importance of industries in generating employment and increasing state revenue. He advises the state to promote industries that produce essential goods and luxury items, both for domestic consumption and export. State run enterprises and monopolies in critical sectors, such as mining and salt production, are also encouraged.

IV. Revenue Generation: A stable and growing economy is essential for generating revenue through taxation. Kautilya's approach to taxation, as discussed earlier, is designed to support economic growth by ensuring taxes are fair, reasonable, and conducive to productive economic activities.

2. Social Growth

I. Education and Knowledge: The Arthashastra highlights the importance of education and the dissemination of knowledge as vital for social growth. Kautilya advocates for state support of educational institutions and the promotion of learning in various fields, including economics, politics, philosophy, and military science.

II. Public Welfare and Social Services: Kautilya emphasizes the state's role in ensuring the welfare of its citizens. This includes providing healthcare, building infrastructure, and maintaining law and order. Social services are seen as essential for creating a stable and productive society, which in turn contributes to overall growth.

III. Justice and Equity: Social growth is also linked to the establishment of a just and equitable society. The Arthashastra advocates for the protection of the vulnerable, fair treatment of all citizens, and the promotion of justice through a well functioning legal system. Ensuring social equity is seen as essential for maintaining harmony and preventing social unrest.

IV. Population Growth and Management: The text acknowledges the role of population growth in the expansion of the state's workforce and military. However, Kautilya also advises measures to manage population growth, ensuring that resources are sufficient to meet the needs of the population.

3. Political and Military Growth

I. Strengthening State Power: Kautilya's vision of growth includes the consolidation and expansion of state power. This involves the efficient administration of the state, the expansion of territories through conquest and diplomacy, and the establishment of a strong central authority.

II. Military Expansion: A powerful and well-equipped military is central to Kautilya's concept of growth. The Arthashastra provides detailed guidelines on building and maintaining a strong army, which is essential for defending the state, expanding its territories, and ensuring internal stability.

III. Diplomacy and Alliances: Diplomatic growth is also emphasized, with Kautilya advising the state to form strategic alliances, engage in treaties, and use diplomacy to achieve its goals. Alliances and good relations with neighbouring states are seen as important for securing peace and facilitating trade.

IV. Internal Security: Political growth is closely tied to the state's ability to maintain internal security. The Arthashastra outlines measures for preventing rebellions, maintaining law and order, and dealing with threats from within the state. A secure state is better positioned to focus on growth and development.

4. Sustainable Growth

I. Resource Management: Kautilya emphasizes the sustainable management of natural resources, such as forests, water bodies, and minerals. He advises the state to ensure that these resources are used efficiently and conserved for future generations. Overexploitation or mismanagement of resources can lead to long term economic decline and social unrest.

II. Balanced Growth: The Arthashastra advocates for balanced growth across different sectors of the economy and regions of the state. This includes promoting both rural and urban development, ensuring that wealth is not concentrated in a few hands, and addressing regional disparities.

III. Crisis Management: Kautilya recognizes the importance of preparing for and managing crises, such as famines, natural disasters, and economic downturns. The state should have contingency plans and reserves in place to mitigate the impact of such events on growth and development.

5. Moral and Ethical Growth

I. Ethical Governance: Kautilya stresses the importance of ethical governance as a foundation for growth. The ruler and state officials are expected to adhere to high moral standards, ensuring that the state is governed justly and effectively. Ethical governance fosters trust, stability, and longterm growth.

II. Promotion of Dharma: The Arthashastra emphasizes the promotion of dharma (righteousness) as a guiding principle for the state. The ruler is responsible for upholding dharma, which includes justice, fairness, and the welfare of the people. A state that adheres to dharma is more likely to achieve sustained growth and prosperity.

III. Public Morality: Social and moral growth is also linked to the promotion of public morality. The Arthashastra advises the state to encourage virtuous behaviour among its citizens, discourage vices such as gambling and alcohol abuse, and maintain social order through a combination of laws and moral education.

6. Innovation and Adaptation

I. Encouragement of Innovation: Kautilya recognizes the importance of innovation and adaptability in achieving growth. The state should encourage new ideas, technologies, and practices that can enhance productivity, efficiency, and overall development. Innovation in agriculture, industry, and administration is particularly emphasized.

II. Adapting to Change: The Arthashastra advises the state to remain adaptable in the face of changing circumstances, whether they are economic, social, or political. This adaptability is crucial for sustaining growth in a dynamic environment. The state should be willing to revise its policies and strategies in response to new challenges and opportunities.

7. Cultural Growth

I. Promotion of Arts and Culture: Kautilya also acknowledges the importance of cultural growth as part of overall development. The Arthashastra advises the state to patronize the arts, literature, and cultural activities. A rich cultural life contributes to the wellbeing of the population and enhances the state's prestige.

II. Preservation of Heritage: The text emphasizes the preservation of cultural heritage and traditions, which are seen as integral to the state's identity and stability. By maintaining cultural continuity, the state can foster a sense of unity and pride among its citizens.

8. Long Term Vision of Growth

I. Sustainable Development: Kautilya's vision of growth is longterm and sustainable, focusing not just on immediate gains but on the enduring prosperity of the state. He advocates for policies that ensure the wellbeing of future generations and the continued strength of the state.

II. Building a Legacy: The Arthashastra encourages rulers to think beyond their own reign and to build a legacy of growth and development that will benefit their successors. This long term perspective is crucial for achieving lasting success and stability.

9. Challenges to Growth

I. Managing Opposition: Kautilya acknowledges that growth often faces opposition, whether from external enemies, internal factions, or economic challenges. The

Arthashastra provides strategies for overcoming these obstacles, including diplomatic, military, and economic measures.

II.   Addressing Corruption: Corruption is seen as a significant impediment to growth. Kautilya emphasizes the need for strict oversight, transparency, and accountability in governance to prevent corruption from undermining the state's development efforts.

10. Conclusion:

I.   Integrated Approach: Kautilya's concept of growth in the Arthashastra is holistic, encompassing economic, social, political, and moral dimensions. Growth is not just about increasing wealth but about creating a stable, just, and prosperous society.

II.   Relevance Today: The principles of growth outlined in the Arthashastra continue to be relevant in modern discussions on development. Kautilya's emphasis on ethical governance, sustainable development, and the balance between economic and social growth offers valuable insights for contemporary policymakers.

In summary, Kautilya's Arthashastra presents a comprehensive vision of growth that integrates economic prosperity, social welfare, political stability, and ethical governance. His approach to growth is strategic and long term, aiming to build a powerful and enduring state.

11. Kautilya's Arthashastra-Oriented Public Expenditure.

In Kautilya's Arthashastra, oriented public expenditure is a key aspect of statecraft, emphasizing the efficient allocation of resources to achieve various objectives related to governance, security, and public welfare. Kautilya (Chanakya) provides detailed guidance on how to manage public funds effectively to support the state's overall goals and ensure the wellbeing of its citizens. The principles of oriented public expenditure in the Arthashastra reflect a strategic approach to using state resources to maximize benefits and maintain stability.

1. Objectives of Public Expenditure

I.   Administrative Efficiency: Public expenditure should be directed towards enhancing the efficiency and effectiveness of the state's administration. This includes funding for bureaucratic functions, maintaining records, and supporting the administrative apparatus.

II.   Military and Defence: A significant portion of public expenditure is allocated to the military and defence. Kautilya emphasizes the importance of maintaining a strong and well-equipped army to protect the state from external threats and ensure internal security.

III.   Infrastructure Development: Investment in infrastructure, such as roads, bridges, ports, and irrigation systems, is crucial for economic growth and stability. Public funds should be used to build and maintain infrastructure that supports trade, agriculture, and overall development.

IV.   Public Welfare: Expenditure on public welfare is essential for maintaining social stability and improving the quality of life for citizens. This includes funding for healthcare, education, and social services to support the wellbeing of the population.

2. Principles of Efficient Public Expenditure

I.   Prioritization of Needs: Kautilya advises that public expenditure should be prioritized based on the state's most pressing needs. Resources should be allocated to areas that will have the greatest impact on the state's stability and growth. For example, funding for defence and infrastructure might take precedence over less urgent expenditures.

II.   Cost Effectiveness: Public expenditure should be managed in a cost-effective manner, ensuring that resources are used efficiently and that expenditures achieve their intended objectives. This involves careful planning, budgeting, and monitoring to prevent wastage and ensure optimal use of funds.

III. Transparency and Accountability: To prevent corruption and misuse of public funds, Kautilya emphasizes the importance of transparency and accountability in public expenditure. Regular audits, oversight, and reporting mechanisms should be established to ensure that funds are used appropriately and that officials are held accountable for their spending decisions.

3. Allocation of Public Funds

I. Administrative Functions: Funds should be allocated to support the administration of justice, law enforcement, and the functioning of government institutions. This includes salaries for officials, maintenance of government buildings, and other administrative expenses.

II. Military Spending: A substantial portion of public expenditure is dedicated to maintaining and expanding the military. This includes costs related to training, equipment, salaries, and fortifications. Kautilya views a strong military as essential for safeguarding the state and achieving its strategic goals.

III. Infrastructure Investment: Investment in infrastructure projects is critical for facilitating trade, agriculture, and overall economic development. Public funds should be used to construct and maintain roads, bridges, irrigation systems, and other critical infrastructure.

IV. Social Welfare Programs: Funding for healthcare, education, and other social welfare programs is necessary for ensuring the wellbeing of the population. Kautilya advocates for the allocation of resources to improve public health, provide educational opportunities, and support vulnerable groups in society.

V. Economic Development Initiatives: Public expenditure should also support initiatives aimed at economic development, such as promoting trade, supporting industries, and encouraging agricultural improvements. This includes subsidies, incentives, and investment in key sectors of the economy.

4. Management of Public Expenditure

I. Budgeting and Planning: Kautilya recommends careful budgeting and planning to ensure that public expenditure aligns with the state's priorities and objectives. A detailed budget should be prepared, outlining expected revenues and expenditures, and adjustments should be made as needed to address changing circumstances.

II. Monitoring and Evaluation: Regular monitoring and evaluation of public expenditure are essential to ensure that funds are used effectively and that expenditures achieve their desired outcomes. Kautilya advises the establishment of mechanisms to track spending, assess the impact of expenditures, and make necessary adjustments.

III. Control Mechanisms: To prevent misuse of funds, control mechanisms such as checks and balances, internal audits, and oversight committees should be implemented. Kautilya emphasizes the need for strict control over public expenditure to maintain integrity and prevent corruption.

5. Crisis Management and Contingency Planning

I. Emergency Funds: Kautilya advises the creation of contingency funds to address unforeseen emergencies, such as natural disasters, wars, or economic crises. These funds should be set aside to ensure that the state can respond effectively to emergencies without disrupting other planned expenditures.

II. Flexible Expenditure: Public expenditure should be flexible enough to adapt to changing conditions. In times of crisis or unexpected events, the state may need to reallocate funds or adjust its expenditure priorities to address urgent needs and mitigate the impact of the crisis.

6. Ethical Considerations in Expenditure

I. Just and Fair Use of Resources: Kautilya emphasizes that public expenditure should be used justly and fairly, with the goal of benefiting the entire population. Resources should be allocated in a way that promotes social equity and supports the common good.

II. Avoidance of Extravagance: The Arthashastra advises against extravagant or unnecessary expenditures that do not contribute to the state's objectives. Public funds should be used judiciously, with a focus on achieving practical and meaningful results.

7. Role of the Ruler in Expenditure Decisions

I. Strategic Oversight: The ruler plays a crucial role in overseeing public expenditure and ensuring that it aligns with the state's strategic goals. Kautilya advises that the ruler should be actively involved in setting expenditure priorities, approving budgets, and monitoring spending.

II. Delegation and Supervision: While the ruler may delegate expenditure decisions to officials and administrators, they must ensure proper supervision and oversight. The ruler's involvement is essential for maintaining accountability and ensuring that public funds are used effectively.

8. Public Perception and Legitimacy

I. Building Trust: Effective management of public expenditure helps build trust and legitimacy for the government. Kautilya recognizes that when citizens see that their resources are being used wisely and for the benefit of society, it enhances the ruler's authority and strengthens the state.

II. Addressing Public Concerns: The state should be responsive to public concerns about expenditure and ensure that spending decisions are transparent and justifiable. Engaging with citizens and addressing their concerns can help maintain public support and stability.

9. Long Term Planning

I. Sustainable Development: Kautilya's approach to public expenditure includes long term planning to support sustainable development. Expenditures should be aligned with the state's long term goals and contribute to the continued growth and stability of the kingdom.

II. Legacy Building: The ruler should consider the long term impact of public expenditure and aim to leave a lasting legacy of development and prosperity. Strategic investments in infrastructure, education, and social welfare can contribute to the state's enduring success.

10. Conclusion: Strategic Approach to Public Expenditure

I. Integrated Strategy: Kautilya's approach to oriented public expenditure is strategic and integrated, focusing on achieving the state's objectives through careful planning, efficient use of resources, and ethical governance.

II. Relevance Today: The principles outlined in the Arthashastra regarding public expenditure continue to be relevant in modern governance. Effective management of public funds, transparency, and strategic allocation are essential for achieving sustainable development and maintaining state stability.

In summary, Kautilya's Arthashastra provides a comprehensive framework for managing public expenditure with a focus on efficiency, fairness, and strategic alignment with state objectives. By prioritizing needs, ensuring transparency, and making informed decisions, the state can effectively use its resources to support growth, security, and public welfare.

12. Kautilya's Arthashastra-Western perspective.

The Arthashastra by Kautilya (Chanakya) is often studied from a Western perspective for its insights into ancient statecraft, political strategy, and economics. The text's relevance and influence have prompted various Western scholars and policymakers to examine its principles and compare them with Western political and economic theories. Here's an overview of how the Arthashastra is perceived and analyzed in Western contexts:

1. Comparative Political Strategy

I.   Realpolitik: Kautilya's approach to politics and statecraft is frequently compared to the concept of Realpolitik in Western political theory. Both emphasize pragmatic, often ruthless strategies to achieve political objectives, prioritize state interests over ethical considerations, and employ manipulation and alliances strategically. Kautilya's emphasis on realworld effectiveness and results parallels the Realpolitik focus on power and practical outcomes.

II. Machiavellianism: Some scholars draw parallels between Kautilya and Niccolò Machiavelli. Both thinkers advocate for a pragmatic approach to governance, where the end justifies the means. While Machiavelli's "The Prince" focuses on maintaining power through shrewdness and political manipulation, Kautilya's Arthashastra addresses broader aspects of governance, including economic management and state security.

2. Economic Theories

I.   Mercantilism and Economics: Kautilya's principles regarding trade, taxation, and resource management are often compared to Western economic theories such as mercantilism. His emphasis on maximizing state revenue, managing resources efficiently, and controlling trade mirrors mercantilist practices aimed at strengthening the state's economic power through regulation and accumulation of wealth.

II. Economic Planning: The Arthashastra's detailed guidelines on economic planning, including infrastructure development and trade facilitation, resonate with modern economic planning principles. Kautilya's strategic approach to economic management, including his views on taxation and public expenditure, provides a historical perspective on issues that are still relevant in contemporary economic policy discussions.

3. Governance and Administration

I.   Administrative Efficiency: The Arthashastra's emphasis on efficient administration and bureaucratic organization is often compared to Western theories of public administration and management. Kautilya's ideas on the roles of various officials, the importance of accountability, and the use of administrative tools align with modern principles of effective governance and public sector management.

II.   Legal and Ethical Dimensions: Western scholars often analyze Kautilya's legal and ethical views in contrast to Western legal philosophies. Kautilya's pragmatic approach to law and justice, which sometimes prioritizes state stability over individual rights, is examined alongside Western legal traditions that emphasize human rights, rule of law, and ethical governance.

4. Military and Strategic Thinking

I.   Military Strategy: Kautilya's military strategies and principles are analyzed in relation to Western military theories. His emphasis on strategic warfare, intelligence, and diplomacy mirrors aspects of modern military strategy and defence planning. His detailed approach to organizing and sustaining a military force is compared with Western strategic doctrines.

II.   Diplomacy and Alliances: Kautilya's views on diplomacy, including the formation of alliances and the use of spies, are often compared to Western diplomatic practices. His strategies for dealing with allies and rivals provide insights into the complexities of international relations and are studied alongside Western diplomatic theories.

5. Ethics and Morality

I.   Ethical Considerations: The Arthashastra's pragmatic approach, which often prioritizes state interests over moral considerations, is contrasted with Western ethical theories that emphasize moral imperatives and the rule of law. Scholars debate the implications of Kautilya's ethical flexibility and its impact on governance and statecraft.

II.   Moral Relativism: Kautilya's acceptance of morally ambiguous tactics for achieving state objectives is analyzed from the perspective of moral relativism. Western scholars explore how Kautilya's pragmatic ethics differ from or align with various ethical frameworks in Western philosophy.

6. Influence and Legacy

I.   Impact on Western Thought: The influence of the Arthashastra on Western political and economic thought is recognized in academic circles. Scholars and policymakers have drawn from Kautilya's work to enrich their understanding of statecraft, economics, and governance.

II. Modern Relevance: The Arthashastra's relevance to contemporary issues in politics, economics, and strategic planning is acknowledged. Western analysts often reference Kautilya's insights to address modern challenges in governance, such as managing resources, navigating international relations, and implementing effective policies.

7. Educational and Scholarly Interest

I.   Academic Study: Western universities and research institutions have increasingly included the Arthashastra in their curriculum, exploring its contributions to political science, economics, and history. Comparative studies between Kautilya and Western theorists provide valuable insights into different approaches to governance and statecraft.

II. Cross Cultural Analysis: The study of the Arthashastra offers opportunities for cross cultural analysis, comparing Eastern and Western approaches to politics and economics. This comparative perspective enriches the understanding of global political and economic systems and their historical development.

8. Criticisms and Interpretations

I.   Criticisms of Pragmatism: Some Western critics argue that Kautilya's pragmatic approach may be too Machiavellian or opportunistic, potentially undermining ethical considerations in governance. This criticism is part of broader debates about the balance between practical effectiveness and moral integrity in statecraft.

II. Different Interpretations: Scholars interpret Kautilya's teachings in various ways, leading to diverse assessments of his contributions. Some view his work as a practical guide to statecraft, while others analyze it as a reflection of the historical and cultural context of ancient India.

In summary, the Arthashastra is analyzed from a Western perspective for its contributions to political strategy, economics, and governance. Its pragmatic approach to statecraft, economic management, and military strategy provides valuable insights that are often compared with Western theories and practices. The text's relevance to contemporary issues and its impact on Western thought highlight its significance in the study of global political and economic systems.

13. Problems in Kautilya's Arthashastra.

Kautilya's Arthashastra is a seminal work on statecraft, economics, and military strategy, but it is not without its problems and criticisms. These issues can be categorized into several areas:

1. Ethical Concerns

I. Machiavellianism: The Arthashastra's pragmatic approach, which often prioritizes state interests over ethical considerations, is viewed as Machiavellian. Its acceptance of deceit, manipulation, and ruthless tactics can be controversial, especially when compared to ethical governance models that emphasize transparency and moral integrity.

II. Moral Flexibility: Kautilya's endorsement of morally ambiguous actions, such as espionage, bribery, and deception, can be criticized for promoting a utilitarian perspective where the end justifies the means. This raises questions about the balance between effectiveness and ethical conduct in leadership.

2. Historical Context and Relevance

I. Ancient Context: The Arthashastra was written in a specific historical and cultural context, which may limit its direct applicability to modern situations. Its recommendations were tailored to the political and social realities of ancient India, which may not align with contemporary political or economic environments.

II. Cultural Bias: Some critics argue that the text's strategies and principles are deeply rooted in the cultural and societal norms of ancient India. This cultural specificity may affect the universal applicability of its ideas and recommendations.

3. Practicality and Feasibility

I. Implementation Challenges: While the Arthashastra provides detailed guidelines on governance and statecraft, the practical implementation of these strategies can be challenging. Some recommendations may be difficult to execute effectively in complex, modern states with diverse political and social landscapes.

II. Resource Constraints: The text assumes that the state has sufficient resources to implement its recommendations, such as maintaining a large military, investing in infrastructure, and funding extensive public services. In reality, resource constraints may limit the feasibility of some of these strategies.

4. Political and Economic Theories

I. Economic Determinism: Kautilya's emphasis on economic control and state intervention in trade and industry reflects a form of economic determinism. Critics argue that this approach may stifle innovation and market dynamics, and may not account for the benefits of free market mechanisms.

II. Centralization of Power: The Arthashastra advocates for a strong, centralized authority with significant control over various aspects of governance and the economy. This centralization can be problematic in terms of balancing power and preventing abuses of authority.

5. Ethical and Social Impact

I. Impact on Society: The focus on state stability and power in the Arthashastra may overshadow the welfare of individual citizens. Strategies that prioritize state interests over social justice and equity could lead to negative social consequences, such as increased inequality and reduced individual freedoms.

II. Exploitation and Coercion: Some of the tactics recommended by Kautilya, such as espionage and coercion, may lead to exploitation and violation of personal freedoms. The ethical implications of these strategies are a point of contention.

6. Ambiguity and Interpretation

I. Ambiguity in Text: The Arthashastra is sometimes criticized for its ambiguous or contradictory passages, which can lead to varied interpretations. This lack of clarity may complicate the application of its principles in practice.

II. Contextual Misinterpretation: Different scholars and practitioners may interpret the text differently, leading to inconsistencies in understanding and applying Kautilya's strategies. This can result in varying assessments of its relevance and effectiveness.

7. Legal and Administrative Issues

I. Legal Framework: The Arthashastra's approach to law and justice may conflict with modern legal standards that emphasize human rights, due process, and the rule of law. Kautilya's focus on maintaining state order through legal and extralegal means may not align with contemporary legal frameworks.

II. Bureaucratic Efficiency: While Kautilya advocates for a well-organized bureaucracy, the practical challenges of implementing and maintaining such a system can be significant. Issues related to corruption, inefficiency, and administrative overload may arise.

8. Diplomatic and Military Strategies

I. Aggressive Tactics: Kautilya's emphasis on aggressive tactics, including subterfuge and military expansion, may be viewed as problematic in modern contexts where diplomacy and conflict resolution are prioritized. The focus on realpolitik and power politics may not align with contemporary values of international cooperation and peaceful coexistence.

II. Balance of Power: The Arthashastra's strategies for balancing power and managing alliances may not fully account for the complexities of modern international relations, where factors such as globalization and interdependence play a significant role.

9. Adaptability to Modern Challenges

I. Contemporary Issues: Some of the Arthashastra's recommendations may not directly address contemporary challenges such as digital security, environmental sustainability, and global economic integration. Adapting its principles to modern contexts requires careful consideration and modification.

II. Technological Advances: The text does not account for technological advancements that have transformed governance, communication, and warfare. Integrating its strategies with modern technology and practices may present challenges.

10. Conclusion: Critical Examination

I. Balancing Perspectives: While the Arthashastra provides valuable insights into ancient statecraft, it is essential to critically examine its principles and adapt them to contemporary contexts. Balancing pragmatic strategies with ethical considerations and modern governance practices is crucial for effective application.

II.   Interdisciplinary Approach: Studying the Arthashastra from an interdisciplinary perspective, considering historical, cultural, and ethical dimensions, can provide a more nuanced understanding of its relevance and limitations.

In summary, Kautilya's Arthashastra, while a significant work on statecraft and governance, faces various problems and criticisms related to its ethical approach, historical context, practicality, and modern applicability. Understanding these issues allows for a more informed and balanced interpretation of its principles and their relevance to contemporary governance and policymaking.

14. Significance of Kautilya's Arthashastra, Arthashastra's Central Theme.

Significance of Kautilya's Arthashastra-

Kautilya's Arthashastra holds a pivotal place in the history of political thought, economics, and statecraft, particularly within the Indian subcontinent, but also globally. Its significance can be understood through several key aspects:

1. Comprehensive Statecraft Manual

I. Holistic Approach: The Arthashastra is one of the earliest comprehensive treatises on governance, covering a wide range of topics including politics, economics, military strategy, law, and social welfare. It serves as a manual for rulers, providing detailed guidelines on how to manage a kingdom effectively.

II. Pragmatism in Governance: The text's pragmatic approach to governance, which emphasizes realworld solutions over idealistic notions, has influenced leaders and policymakers throughout history. It advocates for a ruler who is not only wise and just but also shrewd and strategic.

2. Influence on Indian Political Thought

I. Foundational Text: The Arthashastra is often considered a foundational text in Indian political thought, shaping the development of political philosophy and statecraft in India. It reflects the complexities of governing a large and diverse kingdom and offers insights that are still relevant in modern political discourse.

II. Legacy in Governance: The principles of governance, diplomacy, and administration outlined in the Arthashastra have influenced subsequent rulers and governments in India. Its legacy can be seen in various aspects of Indian administrative practices and political strategies.

3. Contribution to Economic Thought

I. Early Economic Theories: The Arthashastra is one of the earliest works to systematically address economic management, including taxation, trade, market regulation, and resource management. Kautilya's ideas on economic planning and state intervention predate many Western economic theories by centuries.

II.   Public Finance and Taxation: The text provides detailed guidelines on taxation, revenue collection, and public expenditure, laying the groundwork for discussions on public finance and fiscal policy in ancient and medieval India.

4. Strategic and Military Insights

I.   Military Strategy: The Arthashastra offers a sophisticated analysis of military strategy, including the organization of the army, fortification of cities, and the use of spies and intelligence. These strategies are comparable to classical military doctrines and have been studied in the context of both ancient and modern warfare.

II.   Diplomacy and Foreign Policy: Kautilya's insights into diplomacy, including the formation of alliances and the management of foreign relations, have had a lasting impact on the field of international relations. His principles of Realpolitik continue to be relevant in modern geopolitical strategies.

5. Ethical and Legal Philosophy

I.   Ethical Statecraft: While the Arthashastra is often criticized for its pragmatic, sometimes ruthless approach, it also emphasizes the importance of dharma (duty) and the welfare of the people. Kautilya advocates for a ruler who is not only effective but also just and compassionate towards his subjects.

II.   Legal Framework: The text includes a detailed legal code, addressing various aspects of civil, criminal, and administrative law. It provides guidelines for the administration of justice, including the roles of judges, the procedures for trials, and the enforcement of laws.

6. Relevance to Modern Governance

I.   Continuing Influence: The principles outlined in the Arthashastra are still studied and applied in modern contexts, particularly in the fields of political science, economics, and military strategy. Its emphasis on pragmatic governance, economic management, and strategic planning resonates with contemporary policymakers.

II.   Global Recognition: The Arthashastra has gained global recognition as a significant work of ancient literature, contributing to the broader understanding of governance and statecraft in different cultural contexts.

Central Theme of the Arthashastra-

The central theme of the Arthashastra revolves around the comprehensive and pragmatic management of a state, focusing on the pursuit of power, security, and stability. The text is primarily concerned with how a ruler can maintain and expand his kingdom, ensure prosperity, and safeguard against internal and external threats. This overarching theme can be broken down into several core elements:

1. Rajya (The State)

I.   Definition of the State: The Arthashastra defines the state as a complex organization with various interconnected elements, including the king, ministers, the military, the treasury, the territory, and the people. The wellbeing and security of the state are paramount.

II.   Purpose of the State: The primary purpose of the state, according to Kautilya, is to provide security, maintain law and order, promote economic prosperity, and ensure the welfare of its citizens. The state is seen as a mechanism for achieving these goals through effective governance.

2. The King (Ruler)

I.   Role of the King: The ruler, or king, is the central figure in the Arthashastra. The text emphasizes the king's responsibility to govern wisely, protect his subjects, and maintain the stability of the state. The king must be both a warrior and a statesman, capable of making difficult decisions for the greater good.

II.   Qualities of a Good Ruler: Kautilya outlines the qualities of an ideal ruler, including intelligence, discipline, decisiveness, and the ability to inspire loyalty. The king must be both ethical and pragmatic, balancing the demands of power with the welfare of his people.

3. Rajamandala (Circle of States)

I.   Geopolitical Strategy: The concept of the Rajamandala, or the circle of states, is central to Kautilya's foreign policy. It describes a strategic model in which the king's state is surrounded by potential allies, enemies, and neutral states. The king must navigate these relationships through diplomacy, alliances, and, if necessary, warfare.

II.   Balance of Power: The Arthashastra emphasizes the importance of maintaining a balance of power within the Rajamandala. The king must constantly assess the intentions and capabilities of neighboring states to protect his own kingdom and expand his influence.

4. Danda (Authority and Punishment)

I.   Authority and Governance: The concept of danda, or authority, is central to the Arthashastra's vision of governance. The ruler must have the authority to enforce laws, maintain order, and punish wrongdoers. Danda is seen as a tool for ensuring compliance and upholding the rule of law.

II.   Justice and Punishment: The text also addresses the ethical use of danda, emphasizing that punishment should be fair and proportionate. The king must be just in his use of power, balancing severity with compassion to maintain the trust and loyalty of his subjects.

5. Artha (Wealth and Prosperity)

I.   Economic Management: Artha, or wealth, is a crucial theme in the Arthashastra. The text outlines detailed strategies for managing the economy, including taxation, trade, and resource management. Economic prosperity is seen as essential for the stability and strength of the state.

II.   Wealth as a Means to Power: Wealth is not just an end in itself but a means to achieve power and security. The king must ensure the prosperity of his state to maintain a strong military, support public welfare, and secure his rule.

6. Welfare of the People

I.   Public Welfare: While the Arthashastra is often viewed as a text focused on power and control, it also emphasizes the importance of the welfare of the people. The king's ultimate duty is to ensure the wellbeing of his subjects, as a prosperous and contented populace is the foundation of a strong state.

II. Social Order and Justice: The text advocates for the establishment of a just social order, where laws are enforced fairly, and people's rights are protected. The king must balance the needs of different social groups and address the grievances of his subjects.

Conclusion: The central theme of the Arthashastra is the dual pursuit of power and welfare. Kautilya presents a pragmatic vision of governance, where the ruler must be shrewd, strategic, and sometimes ruthless to maintain and expand his kingdom. At the same time, the ruler is expected to be just, ethical, and concerned with the welfare of his people. This balance between realpolitik and dharma (moral duty) is what makes the Arthashastra a timeless and complex work on statecraft.

15. Kautilya's categories of war.

Kautilya, in his Arthashastra, provides a detailed analysis of warfare, categorizing it into several types based on the strategic situation, the objectives of the war, and the means used to conduct it. His classification reflects the pragmatic and strategic nature of his approach to statecraft. The categories of war in the Arthashastra include:

1. Prakasayuddha (Open War)

I. Definition: This is a war that is openly declared and fought in a conventional manner, where both sides are fully aware of each other's intentions. It is a straightforward conflict where the opposing armies meet in the open field.

II. Characteristics: Open war is characterized by direct military engagement, transparency of intentions, and adherence to traditional rules of warfare. It is usually declared after diplomatic negotiations have failed.

2. Kutayuddha (Concealed War)

I. Definition: Also known as a "secret war" or "deceptive war," Kutayuddha involves the use of deception, trickery, and subterfuge. It includes guerrilla tactics, espionage, and psychological warfare.

II. Characteristics: This type of war is characterized by indirect methods, such as spreading misinformation, using spies, or conducting surprise attacks. The goal is to weaken the enemy through covert actions rather than direct confrontation.

3. Tusyayuddha (Silent War)

I. Definition: Tusyayuddha, or "silent war," refers to a conflict that is waged through nonmilitary means, such as economic pressure, diplomatic isolation, or subversion. It is a war of attrition where the objective is to weaken the opponent without open hostilities.

II. Characteristics: Silent war involves tactics like economic sanctions, propaganda, and the creation of internal dissent within the enemy's state. The aim is to undermine the enemy's strength and resolve without direct military action.

4. Mantrayuddha (Diplomatic War)

I. Definition: Mantrayuddha, or "war of counsel," involves the use of diplomacy and negotiation to achieve strategic objectives without resorting to physical conflict. It is a war fought through words, alliances, and treaties.

II. Characteristics: In a diplomatic war, the emphasis is on outmanoeuvring the enemy through strategic alliances, breaking enemy coalitions, and using diplomatic channels to isolate or weaken the opponent.

5. Guerrilla Warfare (Kuta GuptaYuddha)

I. Definition: This type of warfare involves hitandrun tactics, ambushes, and smallscale, irregular skirmishes. It is a form of Kutayuddha but specifically focused on unconventional, irregular warfare.

II. Characteristics: Guerrilla warfare is typically employed by weaker forces against a stronger opponent. It aims to harass and wear down the enemy through persistent, small scale attacks.

6. Dharmayuddha (Righteous War)

I. Definition: Dharmayuddha refers to a war that is fought for a just cause, in accordance with moral and ethical principles. It is waged in the name of duty, justice, or religion.

II. Characteristics: In a righteous war, the combatants adhere to ethical norms and conduct the war in a manner that is considered honorable. The motivation for such a war is often the defence of dharma (righteousness) or protection of the innocent.

7. Akamayuddha (War for Conquest)

I. Definition: Akamayuddha is a war fought with the primary objective of territorial expansion or conquest. It is driven by the desire for power, wealth, and resources.

II. Characteristics: This type of war is characterized by aggressive tactics aimed at subjugating the enemy and annexing their territory. It often involves large scale military campaigns and significant use of force.

8. Lobhayuddha (War for Greed)

I. Definition: Lobhayuddha refers to a war motivated by greed, where the primary objective is the acquisition of wealth or resources rather than territorial expansion or defence.

II. Characteristics: This type of war may involve plundering, looting, or capturing valuable resources such as land, gold, or trade routes. The motivation is purely material gain.

9. Sangramayuddha (Battlefield War)

I. Definition: Sangramayuddha is a conventional battlefield war where large armies clash in open combat. It is the traditional form of warfare involving pitched battles between organized military forces.

II. Characteristics: This type of war is characterized by the use of infantry, cavalry, elephants, and chariots, and is typically fought on predetermined battlefields with clear rules of engagement.

10. Asymmetric Warfare

I. Definition: Although not explicitly named by Kautilya, the concept of asymmetric warfare can be inferred from his discussion of tactics for weaker states or forces. It involves the use of unconventional methods by a weaker power to counteract the strength of a more powerful opponent.

II. Characteristics: Asymmetric warfare includes strategies like sabotage, espionage, and the use of irregular forces to offset the enemy's advantages. It is often employed when direct confrontation is not viable.

Conclusion: Kautilya's categorization of war in the Arthashastra highlights his emphasis on strategic flexibility and adaptability. Rather than prescribing an onesizefitsall approach to conflict, Kautilya recognizes the need for different strategies depending on the context, the strength of the opponents, and the ultimate objectives. His analysis of warfare underscores the importance of understanding the nature of conflict and selecting the appropriate means to achieve victory, whether through direct military engagement, deception, diplomacy, or other methods.

16. Kautilya's Seven Pillars.

Kautilya, in his Arthashastra, outlines a framework known as the "Saptanga" or the "Seven Pillars of the State." These pillars represent the essential components of a stable and prosperous kingdom. Each pillar plays a crucial role in ensuring the effective functioning and longevity of the state. Here's a detailed look at Kautilya's Seven Pillars:

1. Swami (The King)

I. Role: The King is the central figure in the state's governance. He is responsible for the overall welfare of the state, making decisions that affect its prosperity, security, and stability. The king is expected to be wise, just, and capable of making strategic decisions for the good of the people.

II. Qualities: The ideal king is described as disciplined, knowledgeable, and virtuous. He must be able to inspire loyalty among his subjects and maintain a balance between firmness and compassion.

2. Amatya (The Minister)

I. Role: The Amatya refers to the council of ministers who assist the king in the administration of the state. They are responsible for advising the king, implementing policies, and overseeing various aspects of governance.

II. Qualities: Ministers must be competent, loyal, and trustworthy. They should possess administrative skills, be well versed in statecraft, and have the ability to execute the king's orders effectively. The selection of ministers is crucial, as they play a key role in the success or failure of the state.

3. Janapada (The Territory and Population)

I. Role: Janapada represents the land and the people who inhabit it. It includes the kingdom's geography, resources, and population. A prosperous and contented population is vital for the stability and strength of the state.

II. Qualities: The land should be fertile, wellconnected with trade routes, and strategically located to defend against invasions. The population should be industrious, loyal, and diverse in skills, contributing to the economic and military strength of the state.

4. Durga (The Fort)

I.   Role: Durga refers to the fortifications and defensive structures of the state. These include forts, walled cities, and other military installations that protect the kingdom from external threats.

II.   Qualities: A welldesigned and wellmaintained fort is essential for the defence of the state. It should be strategically located, difficult to penetrate, and capable of withstanding sieges. The fort symbolizes the state's strength and ability to protect its people.

5. Kosha (The Treasury)

I.   Role: Kosha represents the state's financial resources, including its treasury, revenue, and wealth. A well-managed treasury is essential for funding the state's administrative functions, military campaigns, and public welfare activities.

II.   Qualities: The treasury should be abundant, ensuring that the state can sustain itself during times of war, natural disasters, or economic downturns. The state should have efficient systems for taxation, revenue collection, and expenditure management.

6. Danda (The Military and Law Enforcement)

I.   Role: Danda refers to the military and law enforcement apparatus of the state. It includes the army, police, and judicial system responsible for maintaining law and order, protecting the state from external aggression, and enforcing the king's authority.

II.   Qualities: The military must be strong, well trained, and loyal to the king. The legal system should be fair and just, with the capacity to enforce laws and punish wrongdoers. The use of Danda (force) should be balanced with justice to ensure the respect and obedience of the population.

7. Mitra (The Allies)

I.   Role: Mitra represents the state's alliances and diplomatic relationships with other states. Allies play a crucial role in providing support during times of war, enhancing trade relations, and helping to maintain a balance of power in the region.

II.   Qualities: Alliances should be formed with states that share common interests and values. The state must carefully choose its allies, ensuring they are reliable and beneficial to its strategic objectives. Diplomacy and negotiation are key skills in maintaining and managing these relationships.

Conclusion: Kautilya's Seven Pillars of the State emphasize the interdependence of various elements of governance. For a state to be strong, all seven pillars must be well maintained and balanced. The king (Swami) is at the center, supported by wise ministers (Amatya), a loyal and productive population (Janapada), strong defences (Durga), a robust treasury (Kosha), a powerful military (Danda), and reliable allies (Mitra). The harmony and effective functioning of these pillars ensure the stability, prosperity, and longevity of the state.

17. Ideology of Kautilya's.

Kautilya's ideology, as presented in his treatise Arthashastra, is a pragmatic and strategic approach to governance, statecraft, and power. It blends elements of realpolitik with ethical considerations, focusing on the effective management of the state while balancing power, economics, and morality. Below are the key aspects of Kautilya's ideology:

1. Pragmatism and Realpolitik

I.   Focus on Power: Kautilya's ideology is centred around the concept of power—its acquisition, maintenance, and expansion. He advocates for a realistic approach to governance, where the pursuit of power is seen as a legitimate and necessary goal for a ruler.

II.   Statecraft: Kautilya views the state as a complex mechanism that requires strategic thinking, careful planning, and sometimes ruthless action to ensure its survival and prosperity. He emphasizes the importance of adapting strategies to the changing political landscape and the capabilities of the state.

2. Rajadharma (Duty of the King)

I.   Moral Responsibility: While Kautilya is often associated with a pragmatic and sometimes ruthless approach, he also stresses the moral responsibility of the king (Rajadharma). The ruler's primary duty is to ensure the welfare of the state and its people. This includes maintaining order, delivering justice, and ensuring economic prosperity.

II.   Ethical Governance: Kautilya advocates for a balance between ethical governance and effective rule. He believes that while power is essential, it should be wielded responsibly, with the ultimate aim of ensuring the welfare of the subjects.

3. Economic Foundations of the State

I.   Artha (Wealth): Central to Kautilya's ideology is the importance of wealth (Artha) as the foundation of a strong state. He argues that economic prosperity is crucial for the state's stability and power, as it enables the funding of the military, public projects, and welfare programs.

II.   Public Finance and Taxation: Kautilya provides detailed guidelines on taxation, revenue collection, and public expenditure. He advocates for a well managed economy where resources are efficiently utilized to benefit the state and its people.

4. Strategic Diplomacy and Warfare

I.   Rajamandala (Circle of States): Kautilya introduces the concept of the Rajamandala, a model for understanding the geopolitical environment. It outlines how a king should manage relationships with neighboring states through alliances, treaties, and, when necessary, warfare.

II.   Types of Warfare: Kautilya classifies different types of warfare, emphasizing the importance of choosing the right strategy based on the state's strengths and weaknesses. He advocates for a mix of open warfare, covert operations, and diplomatic negotiations to achieve the state's objectives.

5. Law and Justice

I.   Danda (Authority and Punishment): Kautilya emphasizes the importance of Danda, or the enforcement of law and order, as a means of maintaining social stability. The ruler must ensure that laws are followed and that justice is administered fairly and effectively.

II.   Legal Framework: The Arthashastra includes a comprehensive legal code that addresses civil, criminal, and administrative law. Kautilya advocates for a legal system that is just but also serves the interests of the state, balancing fairness with the need for authority.

6. Social Order and Welfare

I.   Varna System: Kautilya supports the traditional Varna system, which divides society into different classes (Brahmins, Kshatriyas, Vaishyas, and Shudras). He sees this as a way to maintain social order and ensure that each group contributes to the state's functioning.

II.   Welfare Policies: Despite his focus on power, Kautilya also emphasizes the importance of public welfare. He believes that a prosperous and contented population is crucial for the stability of the state. This includes policies for public health, education, and infrastructure.

7. Realism in Ethics

I. Ends Justify the Means: Kautilya's ideology is often seen as one where the ends justify the means. He advocates for the use of any strategy—be it ethical or unethical—if it ensures the security and prosperity of the state.

II. Balanced Morality: However, Kautilya also acknowledges the importance of maintaining a balance between morality and pragmatism. He suggests that while rulers must be prepared to use harsh measures, they should also strive to be just and compassionate whenever possible.

8. Role of the State

I. Central Authority: Kautilya believes in a strong central authority, where the king holds significant power over all aspects of governance. The state is seen as the primary entity responsible for ensuring order, justice, and prosperity.

II. Interventionist Approach: He supports state intervention in economic and social matters to ensure stability and growth. This includes regulating trade, maintaining public order, and intervening in the market when necessary to protect the state's interests.

Conclusion: Kautilya's ideology, as encapsulated in the Arthashastra, is a sophisticated blend of pragmatism, strategic realism, and ethical governance. While he emphasizes the importance of power and the need for a ruler to be shrewd and sometimes ruthless, he also advocates for the welfare of the people and the ethical use of authority. His ideas on statecraft, economic management, and diplomacy have had a lasting impact on political thought, particularly in the context of governance and leadership in complex and challenging environments.

18. View of Kautilya's about Arthashastra.

Kautilya, also known as Chanakya, viewed the Arthashastra as a comprehensive guide to statecraft, governance, and economic policy. His work reflects a deep understanding of the complexities involved in ruling a kingdom and offers practical advice to rulers on how to maintain power, ensure stability, and promote prosperity. Here's an overview of Kautilya's view on the Arthashastra:

1. A Science of Politics and Economics

1. Arthashastra as a Manual of Statecraft: Kautilya saw the Arthashastra as a systematic and scientific manual for rulers. It provides detailed instructions on how to govern a state effectively, covering areas such as administration, law, military strategy, foreign policy, and economic management. He believed that governance could be approached methodically, and that a ruler could achieve success by following the principles laid out in the text.

2. Focus on Wealth (Artha): The term "Arthashastra" itself signifies the "science of wealth" or "science of material gain." Kautilya emphasized that wealth (Artha) is the foundation of all human endeavors, including statecraft. A strong economy is essential for the security and stability of the state, as it enables the funding of military campaigns, public welfare programs, and infrastructure development.

2. Practicality and Realism

1. Pragmatic Approach: Kautilya's Arthashastra is known for its pragmatic and often ruthless approach to governance. He did not shy away from advocating for the use of any means necessary to achieve the state's objectives, whether they be ethical or not. This includes the use of espionage, manipulation, and even assassination if required for the greater good of the state.

2. Adaptability to Circumstances: Kautilya understood that different situations require different approaches. He emphasized the importance of adaptability and flexibility in governance, advising rulers to assess the situation carefully and choose the most appropriate strategy.

3. Moral and Ethical Dimensions

1. Balance of Morality and Pragmatism: While Kautilya is often seen as a proponent of realpolitik, he also acknowledged the importance of morality and ethics in governance. He believed that a ruler should strive to be just and compassionate, but should not hesitate to take harsh measures when necessary for the state's survival.

2. Rajadharma (Duty of the King): Kautilya placed significant importance on the concept of Rajadharma, or the duty of the king. He believed that the ruler's foremost responsibility was to ensure the welfare of the people and the stability of the state. This includes maintaining law and order, protecting the kingdom from external threats, and ensuring economic prosperity.

4. Comprehensive Governance

1. AllEncompassing Scope: The Arthashastra covers a wide range of topics, making it a comprehensive guide to governance. It includes sections on law, economics, foreign policy, espionage, and military strategy. Kautilya's intention was to provide a ruler with all the necessary knowledge to govern effectively.

2. Detailed Administrative Guidance: Kautilya provided detailed instructions on the administration of the state, including the selection of ministers, management of the treasury, and maintenance of public infrastructure. He believed that efficient administration was crucial for the success of the state.

5. Foreign Policy and Diplomacy

1. Rajamandala Theory: Kautilya introduced the concept of the Rajamandala, or the "circle of states," which outlines the relationships between a king and his neighbours. He viewed foreign policy as a critical aspect of statecraft, emphasizing the importance of alliances, diplomacy, and strategic warfare.

2. Diplomacy as Warfare: For Kautilya, diplomacy was a form of warfare. He believed that a ruler should use diplomacy to weaken enemies, form alliances, and expand influence. His approach to foreign policy was highly strategic, focusing on long term goals and the balance of power.

6. Economic Policy

1. Focus on Wealth Generation: Kautilya viewed economic prosperity as the foundation of a strong state. He provided detailed advice on taxation, trade, and public finance, emphasizing the need for a well-managed economy to support the state's military and administrative functions.

2. Public Welfare: Despite his focus on wealth, Kautilya also stressed the importance of public welfare. He believed that a prosperous and contented population was essential for the stability of the state and advocated for policies that would improve the wellbeing of the people.

Conclusion: Kautilya viewed the Arthashastra as a timeless and practical guide for rulers. He intended it to be a blueprint for building and sustaining a powerful, prosperous, and stable state. The work reflects his deep understanding of human nature, politics, and economics, offering a holistic approach to governance that balances pragmatism with ethical considerations. For Kautilya, the Arthashastra was not just a set of rules but a philosophy of governance that could be adapted to changing circumstances, ensuring the longevity and success of the state.

19. View of Kautilya's Principles of Arthashastra.

Kautilya's principles, as articulated in the Arthashastra, provide a comprehensive guide to governance, economics, and statecraft. His views are grounded in a pragmatic understanding of power dynamics, human behavior, and the complexities of ruling a state. Below is an overview of Kautilya's key principles as reflected in the Arthashastra:

1. The Primacy of Artha (Wealth)

1. Economic Foundation: Kautilya emphasized that economic strength (Artha) is the foundation of a prosperous and stable state. He believed that wealth is essential for the security of the kingdom, as it funds the military, public projects, and administrative functions.
2. State Revenue and Public Finance: One of the central principles is the efficient management of state resources. Kautilya provides detailed guidelines on taxation, trade, and the proper use of public funds to ensure the economic health of the state.

2. Realism and Pragmatism in Governance

1. Power and Statecraft: Kautilya is known for his realistic approach to governance, where the pursuit and maintenance of power are seen as legitimate and necessary. He advocated for a pragmatic approach, where rulers should use whatever means necessary, including espionage, diplomacy, and even deception, to achieve their objectives.
2. Adaptability: A key principle in the Arthashastra is adaptability. Kautilya advises rulers to be flexible and responsive to changing circumstances, whether in times of peace or conflict.

3. Rajadharma (Duty of the King)

1. Moral Responsibility: While Kautilya is often seen as a proponent of realpolitik, he also stresses the ethical responsibilities of a ruler. The king's foremost duty is to ensure the welfare of the state and its people, balancing the pursuit of power with justice and compassion.

2. Justice and Law: Kautilya's principles include the fair administration of justice. He emphasizes the importance of Danda (authority and punishment) in maintaining law and order, but this power must be exercised judiciously and in the interest of the people.

4. Strategic Diplomacy and Foreign Policy

1. Rajamandala Theory: One of Kautilya's key principles is the Rajamandala (Circle of States) theory, which provides a strategic framework for managing relationships with neighboring states. He categorizes states into allies, enemies, and neutral powers, and advises on how to navigate these relationships to maintain a balance of power.

2. Diplomacy as a Tool of War: Kautilya views diplomacy as an extension of warfare. He believes that a wise ruler should use diplomacy to outmanoeuvre opponents, form strategic alliances, and, if necessary, weaken enemies without direct conflict.

5. Ethical Flexibility

1. Ends Justify the Means: A controversial yet central principle in the Arthashastra is the idea that the ends can justify the means, especially when the survival and prosperity of the state are at stake. Kautilya argues that a ruler must be willing to use both ethical and unethical methods if they serve the greater good of the state.

2. Balanced Approach: However, Kautilya also advocates for a balanced approach, where ethical considerations should not be entirely abandoned. He encourages rulers to be just and virtuous, but also to recognize when harsher measures are necessary for the state's survival.

6. Comprehensive Governance

1. Holistic Management: The Arthashastra provides a detailed blueprint for governance, addressing everything from administration and law to military strategy and public welfare. Kautilya's principles are comprehensive, ensuring that all aspects of state functioning are well managed.

2. Efficient Administration: Kautilya emphasizes the importance of a competent and efficient administration. He provides guidelines for the selection of ministers, the organization of the bureaucracy, and the management of public resources.

7. Public Welfare and Social Order

1. Welfare State: Despite his focus on power and strategy, Kautilya also emphasizes the importance of public welfare. He believes that the state should work to improve the wellbeing of its citizens, as a contented and prosperous population is key to the state's stability.

2. Social Order: Kautilya supports the maintenance of social order through the Varna system (caste system), which he sees as a way to ensure that each segment of society contributes to the state's functioning.

8. Military Strength and Security

1. Danda (Authority and Military Power): Kautilya considers military strength essential for the security of the state. He advocates for a well-trained and well-equipped army, capable of defending the state from external threats and maintaining internal order.

2. Use of Force: While Kautilya emphasizes diplomacy and strategic alliances, he also recognizes the necessity of using force when needed. His principles include guidelines for warfare, military tactics, and the strategic use of Danda to enforce the king's authority.

Conclusion: Kautilya's principles, as laid out in the Arthashastra, reflect a sophisticated understanding of statecraft that balances power, ethics, and pragmatism. His approach is both realistic and adaptable, recognizing the complexities of governance and the need for a ruler to be both just and strategically shrewd. The Arthashastra remains a significant text in the study of political philosophy and statecraft, with principles that are applicable beyond its historical context.

20. Administrative ideas in Kautilya's Arthashastra.

Kautilya's Arthashastra is a comprehensive treatise that offers detailed guidelines on the administration of a state. His administrative ideas are focused on ensuring the efficient functioning of the state, maintaining law and order, promoting economic prosperity, and safeguarding the kingdom's security. Below are the key administrative ideas in Kautilya's Arthashastra:

1. Centralized Authority

1. Strong Central Leadership: Kautilya advocates for a strong central authority where the king (Swami) is the supreme ruler and holds ultimate decision making power. The king is responsible for all aspects of governance, and his authority must be respected and upheld by all officials.

2. Council of Ministers (Amatya): The king is advised by a council of ministers, who are selected for their competence, loyalty, and expertise. These ministers play a crucial role in assisting the king in decisionmaking, policy implementation, and the day-to-day administration of the state.

2. Efficient Bureaucracy

1. Structured Administration: The Arthashastra outlines a wellorganized bureaucratic structure with clearly defined roles and responsibilities for various officials. Kautilya emphasizes the importance of appointing capable and trustworthy individuals to key administrative positions.

2. Supervision and Accountability: Kautilya stresses the need for regular supervision and inspection of officials to ensure that they perform their duties effectively. He advocates for a system of checks and balances to prevent corruption and abuse of power, including the use of spies to monitor the conduct of officials.

3. Revenue Collection and Public Finance

1. Taxation System: Kautilya provides detailed guidelines on the collection of taxes, which he sees as the backbone of the state's economy. He recommends a fair and efficient

taxation system that does not overburden the citizens but ensures sufficient revenue for the state's needs.

2. Treasury Management (Kosha): The treasury is central to the administration, and Kautilya emphasizes the importance of prudent financial management. He advocates for the accumulation of wealth in the treasury to fund military campaigns, public works, and welfare programs.

4. Law and Order

1. Legal Framework: The Arthashastra includes an extensive legal code that addresses civil, criminal, and administrative law. Kautilya believes that a well-defined legal system is essential for maintaining order and ensuring justice in society.

2. Danda (Authority and Punishment): Kautilya highlights the importance of enforcing laws through the use of Danda, or punishment, to maintain discipline and order. However, he also stresses that punishment should be just and proportionate to the offense.

5. Public Welfare and Infrastructure

1. Welfare of Citizens: Kautilya emphasizes the king's duty to ensure the welfare of his subjects. This includes providing for public health, education, and economic opportunities. He believes that a contented and prosperous population is crucial for the stability and longevity of the state.

2. Infrastructure Development: The Arthashastra outlines the importance of developing and maintaining public infrastructure, such as roads, irrigation systems, and marketplaces. Kautilya views these as essential for economic growth and the wellbeing of the population.

6. Espionage and Intelligence

1. Network of Spies: Kautilya places significant emphasis on the use of espionage as a tool for maintaining internal security and gathering intelligence. He advocates for a widespread network of spies who monitor both the population and officials, providing the king with valuable information to pre-empt threats and maintain control.

2. Counterintelligence: The Arthashastra also covers counterintelligence measures to protect the state from external spies and subversive activities. Kautilya advises the king to be vigilant against any plots or conspiracies that could destabilize the state.

7. Foreign Relations and Diplomacy

1. Diplomatic Corps: Kautilya outlines the importance of maintaining diplomatic relations with neighbouring states. He provides guidelines for the appointment of envoys and ambassadors who represent the state's interests abroad and negotiate treaties, alliances, and trade agreements.
2. Strategic Alliances: The Arthashastra emphasizes the need for strategic alliances and carefully managed relationships with other states. Kautilya advises the king to use diplomacy, treaties, and marriages to secure the state's interests and avoid unnecessary conflicts.

8. Military Organization

1. Strong Military: Kautilya views a well-organized and disciplined military as essential for the protection and expansion of the state. The Arthashastra provides detailed guidelines on the recruitment, training, and management of the army.
2. Military Strategy: Kautilya also offers advice on military strategy, including the use of fortifications, logistics, and the deployment of troops. He stresses the importance of being prepared for both defensive and offensive operations.

9. Agricultural and Economic Policies

1. Agricultural Management: Recognizing agriculture as the primary source of state revenue, Kautilya advocates for policies that support and protect farmers. He advises the state to provide irrigation facilities, protect crops, and ensure fair trade practices.
2. Trade and Commerce: The Arthashastra emphasizes the importance of promoting trade and commerce for economic growth. Kautilya recommends regulating markets, standardizing weights and measures, and ensuring the availability of essential goods.

Conclusion: Kautilya's administrative ideas in the Arthashastra reflect a comprehensive and systematic approach to governance. His emphasis on a strong central authority, efficient bureaucracy, financial management, law and order, and public welfare provides a blueprint for effective administration. Kautilya's principles are designed to create a stable, prosperous, and secure state, with the king as the central figure responsible for ensuring the wellbeing of the kingdom and its people.

21. Saptanga Theory of Kautilya's Svami, Amaya, Janpada, Durga, Danda, Mitra.

Kautilya's Saptanga Theory, or the Theory of Seven Elements, is a foundational concept in his Arthashastra that outlines the essential components of a state. According to Kautilya, a wellfunctioning and prosperous state is built on these seven elements, each of which plays a critical role in the state's stability, security, and governance. The elements are interdependent, and the health of the state depends on the effective management of each component.

The Seven Elements of the State:-

1. Svami (The King/Ruler)

   1. Role and Importance: The Svami is the central figure in the Saptanga theory, representing the leadership of the state. Kautilya emphasizes that the ruler must be wise, just, and strong, embodying the qualities of a capable leader. The king is responsible for the welfare of the state and its people, and his personal qualities, decision making skills, and vision are crucial for the state's prosperity.
   2. Duties and Responsibilities: The king must ensure good governance, maintain law and order, protect the state from external threats, and promote economic and social welfare. Kautilya also stresses the importance of the king's moral character and the need for him to be guided by ethical principles while being pragmatic in his rule.

2. Amatya (The Ministers/Officials)

   1. Role and Importance: The Amatya represents the administrative machinery of the state, comprising ministers, advisors, and highranking officials. These individuals assist the king in governance and are responsible for the implementation of policies, management of resources, and administration of various state functions.
   2. Selection and Efficiency: Kautilya emphasizes the importance of appointing capable, loyal, and honest ministers who are experts in their respective fields. The effectiveness of the state depends on the efficiency and integrity of these officials, and regular supervision and evaluation of their performance are crucial.

3. Janapada (The Territory/People)

1. Role and Importance: The Janapada represents the state's territory and its people. It includes the land, natural resources, and the population that inhabits the state. Kautilya believed that the prosperity and stability of the state are directly linked to the wellbeing of its people and the fertility of its land.

2. Economic Base: The Janapada is the economic foundation of the state, providing the necessary resources for the state's sustenance, such as agricultural produce, trade, and taxes. Kautilya emphasizes the importance of a prosperous and contented population, as they are the source of the state's wealth and power.

4. Durga (The Fort/Capital)

1. Role and Importance: The Durga refers to the fortified capital city or stronghold of the state. It symbolizes the state's defence and military strength, providing protection against external invasions and internal rebellions. The capital also serves as the administrative and political center of the state.

2. Strategic Importance: Kautilya stresses the need for a well-fortified capital with strong defences, including walls, moats, and watchtowers. The location of the Durga should be strategically chosen to ensure security and control over the surrounding territory.

5. Kosha (The Treasury/Wealth)

1. Role and Importance: The Kosha represents the state's treasury and financial resources. It is the economic backbone of the state, funding the administration, military, public works, and welfare programs. Kautilya believed that a wellmanaged and abundant treasury is essential for the stability and power of the state.

2. Revenue Collection: Kautilya provides detailed guidelines on revenue collection, taxation, and financial management. He emphasizes the importance of accumulating wealth while ensuring that the taxation system is fair and does not burden the population excessively.

6. Danda (The Army/Authority)

1. Role and Importance: The Danda represents the state's military power and the enforcement of law and order. It includes the armed forces as well as the state's ability to

impose authority and punishment (Danda). Kautilya sees a strong and disciplined army as crucial for the protection of the state and the maintenance of internal order.

2. Military Strength: Kautilya advocates for a well-equipped and well-trained military capable of defending the state from external threats and suppressing internal disturbances. The Danda also symbolizes the state's ability to enforce its laws and ensure justice.

7. Mitra (The Allies)

1. Role and Importance: The Mitra refers to the state's allies and diplomatic relations with other states. Kautilya emphasizes the importance of forming strategic alliances to strengthen the state's position and protect it from external threats. Allies can provide military support, economic aid, and political backing.

2. Diplomacy and Foreign Policy: Kautilya advises the king to carefully choose allies based on mutual interests and strategic advantages. Diplomacy, treaties, and marriages can be used to secure alliances, and maintaining good relations with allies is essential for the state's security and expansion.

Interrelation of the Elements:-

Kautilya's Saptanga Theory presents these seven elements as interdependent. The stability and prosperity of the state depend on the harmonious functioning of all seven components. A weakness in any one element can compromise the entire state, so Kautilya emphasizes the need for balanced attention to all aspects of governance.

For example:

A strong Svami (king) is ineffective without competent Amatya (ministers) and a wellmanaged Kosha (treasury).

A prosperous Janapada (territory) requires protection from a well-organized Danda (army) and strategic support from Mitra (allies).

The Durga (capital) serves as the physical embodiment of the state's strength and must be defended by a capable Danda.

Conclusion: Kautilya's Saptanga Theory offers a holistic model of governance where each element of the state is vital for its overall success. By focusing on the interplay between these elements, Kautilya provides a framework for building a strong, prosperous, and enduring state, with a balanced emphasis on leadership, administration, security, economy, and diplomacy.

Unit-II: Economic Thoughts of Kautilya's and It's Contemporary Relevance Thought of Kautilya.

1. Kautilya's A moral politics.

Kautilya, also known as Chanakya, is often perceived as a realist and pragmatist in political thought, especially due to his work in the Arthashastra. However, his approach to politics is not entirely devoid of moral considerations. Kautilya's concept of moral politics involves a delicate balance between pragmatic governance and ethical responsibility, with the ultimate goal of ensuring the welfare of the state and its people.

Key Aspects of Kautilya's Moral Politics:-

1. Rajadharma (Duty of the King)

1. Moral Responsibility: Kautilya emphasizes that the king (Svami) has a moral duty, or Rajadharma, to ensure the welfare of his subjects. The ruler must prioritize the wellbeing, security, and prosperity of the people above all else. While Kautilya advocates for pragmatic and sometimes ruthless strategies, he also insists that the king should act in the best interests of the state and its citizens.

2. Justice and Fairness: Although Kautilya is known for his focus on power and statecraft, he also underscores the importance of justice. The king must be just in his decisions and actions, ensuring that laws are applied fairly and that the rights of individuals are respected. The king's authority is legitimate only as long as it is exercised for the common good.

2. Ethical Flexibility and Realism

1. Ends Justify the Means: Kautilya is often associated with the notion that the ends justify the means, particularly in the context of ensuring the survival and stability of the state. He argues that a ruler may need to employ deception, coercion, or even violence if these actions serve the greater good of the state. However, this pragmatism is not entirely without moral consideration—it is guided by the objective of protecting the state and its people.

2. Pragmatic Morality: Kautilya's moral politics allows for flexibility in ethical decision making, acknowledging that rulers often face complex situations where strict adherence to conventional morality may not be feasible. In such cases, the ruler must weigh the potential outcomes and choose the course of action that minimizes harm and maximizes the benefit to the state.

3. Welfare of the People

1. Public Welfare as a Moral Duty: Kautilya places significant emphasis on the welfare of the people, which he sees as a primary responsibility of the ruler. The state's policies should be designed to improve the living conditions of the population, promote economic prosperity, and ensure social stability. A ruler who neglects the welfare of his people risks losing their loyalty and ultimately undermines the state's stability.

2. Balanced Governance: Kautilya advocates for a balanced approach to governance, where the ruler's pursuit of power is tempered by a commitment to the wellbeing of the people. This includes ensuring access to basic needs, such as food, shelter, and security, and promoting social harmony.

4. Moral Integrity in Leadership

1. Personal Virtue: While Kautilya acknowledges the need for pragmatic decision making, he also recognizes the importance of personal virtue in leadership. A king should possess qualities such as self-discipline, wisdom, and compassion. These virtues help ensure that the ruler's actions are not driven by selfish motives but are aligned with the broader interests of the state.

2. Legitimacy of Rule: The moral integrity of the king is crucial for maintaining the legitimacy of his rule. Kautilya argues that a ruler who acts immorally or unjustly will eventually lose the support of his people and face internal dissent or external threats. Therefore, moral integrity is not only an ethical imperative but also a practical necessity for effective governance.

5. The Role of Danda (Punishment)

1. Just Use of Force: Kautilya views Danda (authority and punishment) as an essential tool for maintaining law and order, but he insists that it must be applied justly and proportionately. The use of force should be directed toward upholding justice and protecting the state, not for personal gain or arbitrary reasons.

2. Ethical Enforcement: The enforcement of laws and the imposition of punishment should be done with fairness and respect for due process. Kautilya emphasizes that excessive or unjust punishment can lead to social unrest and weaken the state's moral authority.

6. Diplomacy and Ethical Conduct

1. Strategic Alliances with a Moral Dimension: In foreign relations, Kautilya advises rulers to form alliances based on mutual benefit and strategic necessity. However, he also suggests that these alliances should be maintained with a degree of moral commitment, honoring agreements and acting with integrity in diplomatic dealings.

2. Ethical Diplomacy: While Kautilya is pragmatic in his approach to diplomacy, he also advocates for maintaining a reputation for reliability and trustworthiness. A ruler who consistently betrays allies or breaks treaties will find it difficult to form new alliances, ultimately weakening the state's position.

Conclusion: Kautilya's moral politics reflects a nuanced understanding of the interplay between ethics and pragmatism in governance. While he acknowledges the complexities and challenges of ruling a state, Kautilya insists that a ruler must strive to balance the pursuit of power with moral responsibility. His approach advocates for a governance model where ethical considerations are integrated into pragmatic decision making, ensuring that the state remains strong, just, and capable of fulfilling its duties to its people.

2. Kautilya's Social Views.

Kautilya, through his work in the Arthashastra, provides insights into the social structure, norms, and values of ancient Indian society. His social views are deeply embedded in the context of the time, reflecting the hierarchical and stratified nature of society, but they also reveal a pragmatic approach to social order, stability, and governance.

Key Social Views in Kautilya's Arthashastra:-

1. Caste System (Varna)

Acceptance of the Caste System: Kautilya's Arthashastra reflects the prevailing social order, which was based on the fourfold Varna system (Brahmins, Kshatriyas, Vaishyas, and Shudras). He accepted the caste system as the foundation of social structure and governance, with each Varna assigned specific duties and responsibilities.

Role of Each Varna:-

1. Brahmins: Kautilya viewed Brahmins as the keepers of knowledge, religion, and moral authority. They were responsible for performing religious rituals, teaching, and advising the king on spiritual and ethical matters.
2. Kshatriyas: The Kshatriyas, or the warrior class, were tasked with ruling, protecting the state, and maintaining law and order. Kautilya placed significant emphasis on their role in governance and military affairs.
3. Vaishyas: The Vaishyas were engaged in trade, agriculture, and commerce. Kautilya saw them as the economic backbone of the state, responsible for generating wealth and contributing to the state's prosperity through taxes.
4. Shudras: The Shudras were primarily labourers and service providers. While they occupied the lowest position in the social hierarchy, Kautilya emphasized the importance of their role in supporting the economy and maintaining the functioning of society.

2. Social Hierarchy and Order

1. Maintenance of Social Order: Kautilya was a strong advocate of social stability and order. He believed that the established social hierarchy was essential for the proper

functioning of the state and society. The duties and responsibilities of each social class were clearly defined to ensure that everyone contributed to the state's wellbeing.

2. Punishment and Regulation: The Arthashastra outlines different punishments for crimes committed by individuals from different social classes, reflecting the hierarchical nature of justice in Kautilya's time. However, Kautilya also stressed that the law should be applied fairly within the context of the social order, to prevent social unrest and ensure that each class fulfilled its duties.

3. Women in Society

1. Role of Women: Kautilya's views on women reflect the patriarchal norms of his time. Women were primarily seen in roles related to the household, family, and domestic responsibilities. However, Kautilya acknowledged the importance of women in maintaining social stability and the household's economic function.

2. Legal Rights and Protections: While women's roles were largely confined to the domestic sphere, Kautilya's Arthashastra does provide some legal protections for women. For example, it includes provisions for the protection of women's property rights, inheritance, and protection against domestic violence. Kautilya also outlines punishments for offenses against women, indicating an awareness of their need for protection within society.

3. Women in Administration: Interestingly, Kautilya's Arthashastra also mentions the employment of women in certain administrative roles, such as spies or agents, where their skills and abilities could be utilized for the state's benefit.

4. Slavery and Labour

1. Slavery: The Arthashastra acknowledges the existence of slavery in society, which was common in ancient times. Kautilya discusses the rights and duties of slaves and slaveowners, indicating that while slavery was accepted, there were regulations in place to govern the treatment of slaves.

2. Labour and Economic Contribution: Kautilya recognized the importance of labour, both free and slave, in the functioning of the economy. He emphasized the need for fair treatment of workers and slaves, ensuring that their labour contributed effectively to the state's prosperity. He also proposed measures for the manumission (release) of slaves

under certain conditions, reflecting a concern for social welfare within the accepted social norms.

5. Religion and Morality

1. Role of Religion: Kautilya viewed religion as a crucial element in maintaining social order and morality. The Arthashastra reflects the integration of religious principles with governance, where religious duties and practices were seen as supporting the moral and ethical framework of society.
2. Religious Tolerance: Kautilya advocated for a degree of religious tolerance, understanding that a ruler should respect the diverse beliefs of the people within the state. He emphasized that the king should protect religious institutions and ensure that religious practices did not lead to social discord.

6. Education and Knowledge

1. Importance of Education: Kautilya placed high value on education, especially for the ruling class and Brahmins. He believed that knowledge was essential for effective governance and moral leadership. Education was also seen as a means of upholding social order by ensuring that individuals were aware of their duties and responsibilities.
2. Training for Governance: The Arthashastra advocates for the systematic training of the king and his ministers in various fields, including administration, economics, warfare, and diplomacy. This emphasis on education reflects Kautilya's belief in the importance of a well-informed and capable leadership.

Conclusion: Kautilya's social views in the Arthashastra are rooted in the context of his time, reflecting the hierarchical and stratified nature of ancient Indian society. However, his approach is pragmatic, focusing on the need for social stability, order, and the effective functioning of the state. While Kautilya accepted the existing social structures, he also advocated for fairness within those structures, promoting the welfare of all classes to ensure the prosperity and security of the state. His social views highlight the balance between maintaining traditional norms and addressing the practical needs of governance.

3. Kautilya's Contract theory of origin of state.

Kautilya's Contract Theory of the Origin of the State is less explicit compared to Western social contract theories, such as those proposed by Hobbes, Locke, or Rousseau. However, Kautilya's Arthashastra offers a view of state formation that implicitly involves a form of social contract, focusing on the roles and agreements between different societal elements.

Kautilya's Implicit Social Contract Theory:-

1. Formation of the State

1. Role of the Ruler: Kautilya believed that a state is formed primarily through the establishment of authority by a powerful ruler. The ruler, or king, emerges as a central figure that organizes and unifies the society. This central authority is crucial for maintaining order, protecting the realm, and ensuring the prosperity of the state.
2. Agreement among People: While Kautilya does not explicitly describe a formal social contract, the idea of the ruler forming an implicit contract with the people can be inferred. In this implicit contract, the people agree to obey and support the ruler in exchange for protection, justice, and economic stability.

2. Mutual Obligations

Ruler's Responsibilities: According to Kautilya, the ruler has several key responsibilities:

1. Protection and Security: The ruler must protect the state from external threats and maintain internal order. This involves both military defence and effective administration.
2. Justice and Fair Governance: The ruler must ensure that laws are applied fairly and that justice is served. The administration of justice is crucial for maintaining the ruler's legitimacy and the stability of the state.
3. Economic Prosperity: The ruler is responsible for promoting economic growth, managing resources efficiently, and ensuring the welfare of the people.

People's Responsibilities: In return, the people have certain obligations:

1. Obedience and Loyalty: The people are expected to obey the ruler's laws and support the state's governance. Their loyalty is crucial for maintaining the stability of the state.

2. Economic Contribution: The people contribute to the state's economy through labour, trade, and taxes. This economic contribution is essential for the state's financial stability and capacity to fulfill its responsibilities.

3. Social Order and Stability

1. Social Structure: Kautilya's theory assumes a hierarchical social structure, where each class or group has specific roles and responsibilities. The social order is maintained through the ruler's authority and the adherence of people to their prescribed roles.
2. Regulation and Control: The ruler has the authority to implement regulations and control mechanisms to ensure social stability. This includes the use of law, punishment, and surveillance to maintain order and prevent dissent.

4. Legitimacy of Authority

1. Consent and Legitimacy: While Kautilya does not explicitly discuss the concept of consent as in Western social contract theories, the legitimacy of the ruler's authority depends on their ability to fulfil their responsibilities effectively. If the ruler fails to provide protection, justice, or economic stability, their legitimacy is undermined, leading to potential unrest or rebellion.
2. Public Welfare: The ruler's legitimacy is also linked to their commitment to the welfare of the people. Kautilya emphasizes that a ruler who fails to ensure the wellbeing of the population risks losing their support and authority.

5. Pragmatic Realism

1. Realpolitik Approach: Kautilya's approach to state formation is pragmatic and realistic. He acknowledges the complexities of governance and the need for strategic and sometimes ruthless actions to maintain the state's stability and power. This pragmatic approach reflects an understanding that the formation and maintenance of the state involve both formal agreements and practical realities.

Conclusion: Kautilya's views on the origin and formation of the state in the Arthashastra do not explicitly outline a formal social contract but rather reflect an implicit understanding of mutual obligations between the ruler and the people. The ruler, emerging as a central authority, establishes the state through their ability to organize and govern effectively. In return, the people agree to support the ruler and contribute to the state's economy and stability. This implicit contract is based on the ruler's ability to provide protection, justice, and prosperity, ensuring the legitimacy of their authority and the stability of the state.

4. Kautilya's Nature state.

Kautilya's view of the nature of the state is intricately described in his seminal work, the Arthashastra. His perspective is rooted in a pragmatic and often realistic understanding of political power, governance, and statecraft. Here's a comprehensive look at Kautilya's concept of the state:

1. The State as a Political Entity

I.   Central Authority: According to Kautilya, the state is a centralized political entity that exists to maintain order, protect its territory, and ensure the welfare of its people. The central authority, usually represented by the king (Svami), is crucial in organizing and governing the state.

II.   Functional Role: The state's primary functions include maintaining law and order, managing resources, conducting diplomacy, and defending against external threats. The ruler's role is to oversee these functions and ensure the effective administration of the state.

2. Realist Perspective

I.   Power and Pragmatism: Kautilya's view of the state is deeply realist. He emphasizes the importance of power, strategy, and pragmatism in governance. The ruler must be adept in political manoeuvring, diplomacy, and sometimes even ruthless actions to secure and maintain power.

II.   Political Stability: The stability and strength of the state are paramount. Kautilya argues that maintaining control over the state requires a ruler who can make pragmatic decisions, including the use of espionage, alliances, and, if necessary, coercion and deception.

3. Theories of State Formation

I.   Saptanga (Seven Pillars): Kautilya describes the state as being composed of seven essential elements or pillars: the king (Svami), the ministers (Amatya), the territory and people (Janapada), the fort or capital (Durga), the treasury (Kosha), the army (Danda), and the allies (Mitra). Each of these elements plays a critical role in the functioning and stability of the state.

II.   Saptanga Theory: The interdependence of these elements underscores the complexity of statecraft. The effectiveness of one pillar impacts the overall strength and stability of the state. For instance, a strong army (Danda) is crucial for defence, while a well-managed treasury (Kosha) supports the state's financial stability.

4. Role of the Ruler

I.   Leadership and Authority: The king is the central figure in Kautilya's conception of the state. The ruler's ability to govern effectively is essential for the state's success. The king must be wise, strategic, and capable of making difficult decisions for the good of the state.

II.   Moral and Practical Leadership: While Kautilya acknowledges the need for pragmatism, he also recognizes the importance of moral leadership. The ruler must balance practical governance with ethical considerations to maintain legitimacy and stability.

5. Functionality and Organization

I.   Administration and Bureaucracy: Kautilya emphasizes the importance of a well-organized administration and efficient bureaucracy. Effective governance requires a structured approach to administration, with clearly defined roles and responsibilities for various officials and ministers.

II.   Economic Management: The state's economic health is critical for its stability. Kautilya outlines strategies for managing the economy, including taxation, trade, and resource management, to ensure the state's prosperity.

6. Diplomacy and Warfare

I.   Strategic Diplomacy: Kautilya places significant emphasis on the role of diplomacy in statecraft. Forming strategic alliances, negotiating treaties, and leveraging political relationships are vital for the state's security and expansion.

II.   Warfare and Defence: Warfare is also a crucial aspect of Kautilya's view of the state. The ruler must be prepared for both defensive and offensive strategies to protect and enhance the state's position. The management of military resources and strategic planning are key components of statecraft.

7. Ethical and Moral Dimensions

I.   Pragmatic Ethics: Kautilya's approach to statecraft includes a pragmatic view of ethics. He acknowledges that rulers may need to employ deception or manipulation to achieve their goals. However, these actions are justified if they serve the greater good of the state.

II.   Welfare and Justice: Despite his pragmatic approach, Kautilya also stresses the importance of ensuring the welfare of the people and maintaining justice. The ruler's legitimacy is tied to their ability to provide for the population and uphold social order.

Conclusion: Kautilya's view of the nature of the state in the Arthashastra presents a complex and pragmatic understanding of governance. The state is seen as a central authority that requires effective leadership, strategic management, and a balance between power and ethics. The ruler's role is pivotal in ensuring the state's stability, prosperity, and security, with the state functioning as a dynamic and multifaceted entity. Kautilya's emphasis on practical strategies, effective administration, and the interplay of various elements reflects his deep understanding of the challenges and realities of statecraft.

5. Kautilya's Welfare state.

Kautilya's concept of a welfare state in his treatise, the Arthashastra, reflects a pragmatic approach to governance that aims to ensure the wellbeing and stability of the state and its people. While Kautilya's welfare state is not framed in the modern sense of the term, his ideas about state responsibility and public welfare are integral to his overall political philosophy.

Key Aspects of Kautilya's Welfare State-

1. Ruler's Responsibility

I. Duty to Protect and Provide: Kautilya emphasizes that the ruler has a fundamental duty to protect the state and ensure the welfare of its people. This includes safeguarding the population from external threats, maintaining internal order, and promoting economic prosperity.

II. Public Welfare: The ruler's legitimacy is closely tied to their ability to ensure the wellbeing of the citizens. Kautilya stresses that a ruler who fails to address the needs and concerns of the populace risks losing their support and undermining the stability of the state.

2. Economic Management

I. Resource Allocation: Effective management of the state's resources is crucial for public welfare. Kautilya discusses various methods for managing resources, including taxation, trade regulation, and economic planning, to ensure that the state's wealth is used for the benefit of its citizens.

II. Agriculture and Trade: Kautilya recognizes the importance of agriculture and trade in supporting the state's economy. Policies that promote agricultural productivity and facilitate trade are seen as essential for ensuring the economic stability and prosperity of the state.

3. Law and Justice

I. Legal Framework: The Arthashastra outlines a legal framework aimed at maintaining order and justice. Kautilya advocates for a system of laws that apply fairly and consistently, ensuring that justice is served and disputes are resolved equitably.

II. Punishment and Rehabilitation: Kautilya discusses the use of punishment as a means to maintain social order, but he also emphasizes the need for a balanced approach that avoids excessive cruelty. Rehabilitation and fair treatment of offenders are important for maintaining social harmony.

4. Social Stability

I. Social Order: Kautilya's welfare state includes measures to maintain social stability and order. This involves regulating social conduct, managing conflicts, and ensuring that societal norms and roles are respected.

II. Public Infrastructure: The development and maintenance of public infrastructure, such as roads, markets, and fortifications, are crucial for the efficient functioning of the state and the welfare of its people. Kautilya acknowledges the importance of investing in infrastructure to support economic activities and ensure public safety.

5. Education and Knowledge

I. Importance of Education: Kautilya places value on education as a means of promoting knowledge and skill development. Education is seen as a key factor in producing competent administrators and leaders, which in turn supports the welfare of the state.

II. Training for Governance: The training of officials and administrators in various aspects of governance, including economics, law, and military strategy, is essential for effective state management and public welfare.

6. Healthcare and Public Health

I. Healthcare Measures: While the Arthashastra does not explicitly focus on modern concepts of public health, Kautilya acknowledges the importance of maintaining the health of the population. Ensuring access to basic healthcare and managing public health issues are implied as part of the ruler's responsibilities.

II. Sanitation and Hygiene: The management of sanitation and hygiene is important for preventing disease and maintaining public health. Although not detailed extensively, Kautilya's emphasis on a well-managed state suggests a concern for basic health and sanitation measures.

7. Economic Equity and Social Welfare

I. Economic Policies: Kautilya's economic policies are designed to create a stable and prosperous economy, which contributes to social welfare. This includes regulating markets, ensuring fair trade practices, and managing resources to prevent economic disparities.

II. Support for the Vulnerable: Although not explicitly outlined as a modern welfare program, Kautilya's emphasis on public welfare implies a concern for the vulnerable segments of society. Ensuring that the basic needs of all citizens are met contributes to the overall stability and harmony of the state.

Conclusion: Kautilya's concept of a welfare state in the Arthashastra reflects a pragmatic and holistic approach to governance. The ruler's primary responsibility is to ensure the wellbeing of the people by managing resources effectively, maintaining social order, and promoting economic prosperity. While not framed in the modern sense of welfare state concepts, Kautilya's ideas emphasize the importance of addressing public needs, ensuring justice, and investing in infrastructure and education to support the overall stability and prosperity of the state.

6. Kautilya's King.

In Kautilya's Arthashastra, the concept of the king (Svami) is central to his political philosophy and statecraft. Kautilya's portrayal of the king reflects a blend of strategic realism, moral considerations, and practical governance. Here's an in-depth look at Kautilya's view of the king:

1. Central Role and Authority

I.   Supreme Authority: The king is the central authority in Kautilya's political system. He holds supreme power over all aspects of governance, including administration, military strategy, law enforcement, and economic management. The stability and effectiveness of the state largely depend on the king's ability to exercise this power judiciously.

II.   Symbol of Unity: The king symbolizes the unity and continuity of the state. His leadership is crucial in maintaining internal coherence and external strength.

2. Qualities of an Ideal King

I.   Wisdom and Intelligence: Kautilya emphasizes the importance of wisdom and intelligence for a king. The ruler must be knowledgeable about various aspects of governance, including politics, economics, and military strategy.

II.   Strategic Acumen: The king should possess strategic acumen, capable of making prudent decisions in both domestic and foreign affairs. This includes forming alliances, conducting diplomacy, and managing conflicts effectively.

III.   Pragmatism: Kautilya advocates for a pragmatic approach to governance. The king should be able to adapt to changing circumstances and employ practical solutions, even if they involve deception or manipulation, to achieve the state's objectives.

IV.   Ethical Conduct: While Kautilya is known for his pragmatic and sometimes ruthless advice, he also acknowledges the importance of ethical conduct. The king's actions should ultimately serve the greater good of the state and its people.

3. Responsibilities and Duties

I. Protection and Security: One of the primary responsibilities of the king is to ensure the protection and security of the state. This involves defending against external threats, maintaining internal order, and safeguarding the population.

II. Justice and Law: The king is responsible for upholding justice and ensuring that laws are applied fairly. Kautilya outlines a legal framework that the king must enforce to maintain social order and prevent injustice.

III. Economic Management: The king must manage the state's economic resources efficiently. This includes overseeing taxation, trade, agriculture, and resource allocation to ensure the prosperity and stability of the state.

IV. Public Welfare: The king has a duty to promote the welfare of the people. This involves addressing their needs, ensuring economic stability, and providing for their basic necessities.

4. Governance and Administration

I. Bureaucratic Structure: Kautilya emphasizes the importance of a well-organized bureaucracy to assist the king in governance. The king should appoint capable ministers and officials to manage various aspects of administration effectively.

II. Advisors and Spies: The king is advised to employ spies and advisors to gather intelligence and provide counsel. This helps the ruler make informed decisions and stay aware of internal and external developments.

5. Diplomacy and Warfare

I. Diplomatic Skills: The king should be adept in diplomacy, forming alliances and negotiating treaties to strengthen the state's position. Kautilya views diplomacy as a crucial tool for maintaining peace and securing advantages in international relations.

II. Military Leadership: The king must also be an effective military leader, capable of commanding the army and implementing strategies for defence and expansion. Military prowess is essential for protecting the state and asserting its power.

6. Moral and Ethical Considerations

I.   Moral Pragmatism: Kautilya's advice often reflects a pragmatic approach to ethics. While the king is expected to act in ways that promote the state's stability and prosperity, this may involve morally ambiguous actions, such as deception or manipulation.

II.   Legitimacy and Trust: The king's legitimacy is closely tied to his ability to provide for the people and uphold justice. Despite the pragmatic approach, maintaining the trust and support of the populace is essential for the ruler's continued authority.

7. Challenges and Threats

I.   Internal Dissent: The king must address internal dissent and manage potential threats to his authority. This involves balancing the interests of different social groups and addressing grievances to prevent rebellion.

II.   External Threats: The king must also prepare for external threats, including invasions and conflicts with rival states. Strategic planning and military preparedness are critical for defending the state's territory and interests.

Conclusion: Kautilya's view of the king in the Arthashastra presents a complex and multifaceted role, blending strategic acumen with ethical considerations. The king is seen as the central figure in maintaining the state's stability, prosperity, and security. While Kautilya's advice emphasizes pragmatic and sometimes ruthless strategies, it also underscores the importance of wisdom, justice, and effective governance. The ruler's success depends on his ability to balance these aspects and fulfil his responsibilities to the state and its people.

7. Kautilya's Kosh. (Treasury)

In Kautilya's Arthashastra, the Kosh (or Kosha) refers to the state treasury and is a crucial component in the administration and economic management of the state. The treasury is not merely a repository of wealth but a vital instrument for sustaining the state's operations, ensuring stability, and enabling governance.

Key Aspects of the Kosh (Treasury) in Kautilya's Arthashastra-

1. Importance of the Treasury

I. Central Role: The Kosh is central to the functioning of the state. It provides the financial resources necessary for administration, defence, public works, and other state functions. Effective management of the treasury is critical for the stability and prosperity of the state.

II. Economic Foundation: The health of the treasury reflects the economic stability of the state. A well-managed Kosh ensures that the state can meet its financial obligations and invest in its development.

2. Sources of Revenue

I. Taxes: Taxes are a primary source of revenue for the Kosh. Kautilya outlines various forms of taxation, including land taxes, trade taxes, and duties. Efficient tax collection and administration are essential for maintaining a robust treasury.

II. Trade and Commerce: Revenue from trade and commerce contributes significantly to the treasury. Kautilya emphasizes the importance of regulating and promoting trade to enhance the state's financial resources.

III. Resource Management: The state's natural resources, such as minerals, forests, and agricultural produce, are also sources of revenue. Proper management and utilization of these resources are crucial for maximizing income for the treasury.

3. Management and Administration

I. Treasury Officials: The management of the Kosh involves appointed officials who oversee the collection, storage, and disbursement of funds. These officials must be competent and trustworthy to ensure the efficient operation of the treasury.

II. Accounting and Auditing: Kautilya stresses the importance of accurate accounting and auditing to prevent corruption and mismanagement. Regular audits help maintain transparency and accountability in the management of state finances.

4. Utilization of Funds

I. Administrative Expenses: Funds from the treasury are used to cover the costs of administration, including the salaries of officials, maintenance of infrastructure, and other operational expenses.

II. Military and Defence: A significant portion of the treasury is allocated to defence and military expenditures. This includes funding for the army, fortifications, and other defence related activities.

III. Public Welfare and Infrastructure: Investment in public welfare, such as healthcare, education, and infrastructure projects, is also funded by the treasury. Kautilya recognizes the importance of these expenditures for maintaining social stability and promoting economic growth.

5. Economic Policy and Planning

I. Budgeting and Planning: Effective budgeting and financial planning are essential for managing the Kosh. Kautilya advises on strategic allocation of resources to ensure that the state can meet its needs and achieve its goals.

II. Debt Management: Managing state debt and financial obligations is a critical aspect of treasury management. Kautilya provides guidance on handling state debt and ensuring that borrowing does not jeopardize the state's financial stability.

6. Challenges and Risks

I. Corruption and Theft: The treasury is susceptible to risks such as corruption, theft, and mismanagement. Kautilya advises on measures to prevent and address these issues, including stringent oversight and penalties for officials who misuse their authority.

II. Economic Fluctuations: Economic fluctuations and external factors can impact the treasury's stability. Kautilya suggests strategies for mitigating these risks, such as diversifying sources of revenue and maintaining financial reserves.

7. Strategic Importance

I. Power and Influence: Control over the treasury enhances the ruler's power and influence. A well-founded treasury allows the state to exert its influence, forge alliances, and project power both domestically and internationally.

II. State Stability: The stability and effectiveness of the treasury are directly linked to the overall stability of the state. A strong and wellmanaged Kosh contributes to a stable and prosperous governance structure.

Conclusion: In the Arthashastra, the Kosh (treasury) is a pillar of governance, essential for the effective functioning and stability of the state. Kautilya's detailed guidelines on the management of the treasury reflect its critical role in supporting administration, defence, and public welfare. The treasury's health and efficiency are central to the state's economic stability and its ability to meet its obligations and objectives. Kautilya's emphasis on prudent management, accountability, and strategic planning highlights the importance of the Kosh in maintaining the prosperity and power of the state.

8. Kautilya's Danda.

In Kautilya's Arthashastra, the concept of Danda (often translated as "punishment" or "authority") is one of the seven pillars of the state, known as the Saptanga. Danda plays a crucial role in the administration and governance of the state. It encompasses not just punitive measures but also the broader concept of state authority and enforcement mechanisms.

Key Aspects of Danda in Kautilya's Arthashastra-

1. Definition and Scope

    I.   Punishment and Authority: Danda refers to the use of authority and punishment to maintain law and order. It involves the enforcement of laws, administration of justice, and implementation of state policies. While often associated with punitive measures, it also encompasses the broader exercise of state power.

    II.   Enforcement Mechanism: As a pillar of the state, Danda represents the mechanisms through which the state enforces its rules, maintains discipline, and ensures compliance with laws and policies.

2. Role in Governance

    I.   Maintaining Order: Danda is crucial for maintaining internal order and stability. By enforcing laws and implementing punishments for transgressions, the state ensures that societal norms are upheld and that individuals adhere to legal and moral standards.

    II.   Upholding Justice: The administration of justice is a key function of Danda. It involves adjudicating disputes, addressing grievances, and imposing penalties for criminal behaviour. Effective justice administration is essential for maintaining social harmony and the ruler's legitimacy.

3. Components of Danda

    I.   Law Enforcement: Danda includes the activities of law enforcement agencies and officials responsible for upholding laws and regulations. This may involve the police, judiciary, and other administrative bodies.

II. Punishment: Punishments for crimes and violations are a direct application of Danda. These can range from fines and confiscation of property to more severe penalties such as imprisonment or execution. The severity of punishment is intended to deter criminal behaviour and maintain discipline.

4. Strategic Use of Danda

I. Deterrence: The effective use of Danda serves as a deterrent to potential offenders. By ensuring that the consequences of illegal or immoral actions are clear and consistently enforced, the state discourages people from engaging in criminal activities.

II. Control and Compliance: Danda helps in controlling the population and ensuring compliance with state policies. It reinforces the ruler's authority and the state's power to govern effectively.

5. Balancing Authority and Justice

I. Proportionality: Kautilya emphasizes the need for proportionality in punishment. The severity of the penalty should match the seriousness of the offense. This ensures that justice is served fairly and avoids excessive cruelty.

II. Ethical Considerations: While Danda involves the use of authority and punishment, Kautilya also acknowledges the importance of ethical considerations. The ruler must balance the need for enforcement with the principles of justice and fairness to maintain legitimacy and public trust.

6. Administration and Implementation

I. Efficient Machinery: The effective implementation of Danda requires a well-organized administrative machinery. This includes trained officials, an efficient legal system, and proper infrastructure for law enforcement.

II. Monitoring and Oversight: Regular monitoring and oversight are essential to ensure that Danda is applied correctly and that officials do not abuse their power. Kautilya advises on maintaining checks and balances to prevent corruption and misuse.

7. Danda in Diplomacy and Warfare

I.   Military Enforcement: Danda also encompasses the use of military force to enforce state authority and defend the state. The ruler must be prepared to use military power to maintain internal order and protect against external threats.

II.   Diplomatic Leverage: In diplomatic relations, Danda can be used strategically to project power and influence. The ability to enforce laws and maintain order enhances the state's negotiating position and credibility.

Conclusion: In the Arthashastra, Danda represents a fundamental aspect of governance, encompassing both the authority of the state and its mechanisms for enforcement and punishment. It plays a critical role in maintaining order, upholding justice, and ensuring compliance with state laws and policies. Kautilya's detailed treatment of Danda highlights its importance in the effective functioning of the state and the ruler's ability to govern effectively. The concept reflects a balance between authority and justice, emphasizing the need for both strategic enforcement and ethical considerations in statecraft.

9. Kautilya's Durg.

In Kautilya's Arthashastra, the term Durga (often translated as "fort" or "fortification") is one of the seven pillars of the state, known as the Saptanga. The concept of Durga is crucial for understanding the strategic and defensive aspects of governance according to Kautilya. It represents both the physical fortifications of the state and the broader concept of the state's defensive and protective mechanisms.

Key Aspects of Durga in Kautilya's Arthashastra-

1. Definition and Scope

I. Physical Fortifications: Durga primarily refers to physical fortifications such as cities, fortresses, and defensive walls that protect the state from external threats. These structures are essential for safeguarding the state's territory and maintaining security.

II. Defensive Measures: Beyond physical fortifications, Durga also encompasses various defensive measures and strategies employed to protect the state from invasions, attacks, and other security threats.

2. Importance in Governance

I. Security and Defence: Durga plays a critical role in ensuring the security and defence of the state. Effective fortifications and defensive strategies help prevent invasions and protect the state's sovereignty.

II. Strategic Advantage: Well-designed and well-maintained fortifications provide a strategic advantage in warfare and conflict. They can serve as strongholds from which the state can launch offensives or defend against attacks.

3. Components of Durga

I. City Fortifications: This includes walls, moats, and gates that protect urban centres. Fortified cities are designed to withstand sieges and attacks, providing a safe haven for the population and resources.

II.   Military Defences: The state must also maintain a strong military presence and infrastructure to support its fortifications. This includes training soldiers, managing supplies, and ensuring readiness for defence operations.

4. Strategic Considerations

I.   Location and Design: The strategic location and design of fortifications are crucial. Kautilya advises on selecting locations that offer natural advantages, such as high ground or difficult terrain, and designing fortifications that enhance defensive capabilities.

II.   Maintenance and Improvement: Regular maintenance and improvement of fortifications are essential for ensuring their effectiveness. This includes repairing and upgrading structures to address vulnerabilities and adapt to changing military technologies and tactics.

5. Role in Administration

I.   Control and Administration: Fortifications also play a role in administrative control. They help manage and regulate the movement of people and goods, maintain order, and enforce laws within the state's territory.

II.   Resource Management: The fortifications and their associated infrastructure require resources for construction, maintenance, and operation. Effective management of these resources is essential for sustaining the state's defensive capabilities.

6. Psychological Impact

I.   Deterrence: Well-fortified cities and strong defensive structures can act as a deterrent to potential aggressors. The presence of formidable defences may discourage attacks and reduce the likelihood of conflict.

II.   Morale: The security provided by fortifications contributes to the morale of the population and the military. Knowing that the state is well defended enhances confidence and stability.

7. Economic and Social Aspects

I. Economic Impact: The construction and maintenance of fortifications have economic implications. Resources spent on fortifications could otherwise be used for development or welfare. Kautilya advises balancing defensive expenditures with other state needs.

II. Social Organization: Fortifications influence social organization within the state. They shape the layout of cities, influence settlement patterns, and impact the daily lives of the population.

Conclusion: In the Arthashastra, Durga (fortifications) is a vital component of statecraft, encompassing both physical defences and broader strategic measures for maintaining security. Effective fortifications are essential for protecting the state from external threats, providing a strategic advantage in conflict, and ensuring the stability and safety of the state's territory. Kautilya's focus on Durga highlights the importance of strategic planning, maintenance, and the integration of defensive measures into the overall governance and administration of the state.

10. Kautilya's Janpad.

In Kautilya's Arthashastra, the term Janpad refers to the geographical and administrative unit of the state, encompassing the territory, population, and resources within its boundaries. It is one of the seven pillars of the state, known as the Saptanga. Understanding the Janpad is crucial for grasping Kautilya's perspective on state administration and territorial management.

Key Aspects of Janpad in Kautilya's Arthashastra-

1. Definition and Scope

    I.   Geographical Unit: Janpad represents the territorial area under the state's control, including its cities, towns, villages, and natural resources. It is the physical space where the state's administration and governance activities take place.

    II.   Administrative Division: Within the broader state, Janpad functions as an administrative unit responsible for local governance and management. It plays a role in implementing state policies and maintaining order within its jurisdiction.

2. Importance in Governance

    I.   Resource Management: Effective management of the Janpad is crucial for utilizing and conserving the state's natural resources, such as land, water, minerals, and forests. Proper resource management supports economic stability and growth.

    II.   Population Administration: The Janpad includes the state's population, and managing it involves addressing the needs and concerns of residents, ensuring their welfare, and maintaining social order.

3. Components of Janpad

    I.   Territory and Boundaries: The physical territory of the Janpad includes its geographical features and boundaries. Clear delineation of these boundaries is essential for administrative clarity and effective governance.

    II.   Local Governance: The Janpad is administered by local officials or administrators appointed by the central government. These officials are responsible for implementing state policies, collecting taxes, and managing local affairs.

4. Strategic and Administrative Considerations

I. Strategic Location: The strategic location of the Janpad can influence its importance in terms of defence, trade, and economic activities. Kautilya advises on leveraging geographical advantages for strategic benefits.

II. Administrative Efficiency: Efficient administration within the Janpad involves organizing local resources, infrastructure, and personnel to ensure effective governance and service delivery.

5. Economic and Social Aspects

I. Economic Activities: The Janpad encompasses various economic activities, including agriculture, trade, and industry. Managing these activities effectively contributes to the state's economic prosperity.

II. Social Organization: Social structures and organization within the Janpad affect governance and administration. Understanding local social dynamics helps in addressing issues related to law, order, and public welfare.

6. Revenue and Taxation

I. Tax Collection: The Janpad plays a role in tax collection and revenue generation for the state. Local officials are responsible for assessing and collecting taxes from the population and businesses within their jurisdiction.

II. Resource Allocation: Revenue generated from the Janpad supports local infrastructure, public services, and development projects. Effective allocation of resources ensures balanced regional development.

7. Challenges and Management

I. Internal Conflicts: Managing internal conflicts and disputes within the Janpad is essential for maintaining order and stability. Local officials must address grievances and resolve conflicts to prevent unrest.

II. Natural Disasters: The Janpad may face challenges related to natural disasters, such as floods, droughts, or earthquakes. Effective management and disaster preparedness are crucial for mitigating the impact of such events.

8. Integration with the State

I. Coordination with Central Government: The Janpad operates within the framework set by the central government. Coordination between local administrators and the central authority ensures the alignment of local and state level policies.

II. Implementation of Policies: Local officials in the Janpad are responsible for implementing state policies and regulations. Their effectiveness in this role impacts the overall governance and administration of the state.

Conclusion: In the Arthashastra, Janpad represents a critical element of the state's territorial and administrative framework. It encompasses the geographical area, population, and resources under the state's control, playing a vital role in governance, resource management, and local administration. Kautilya's focus on Janpad highlights the importance of effective management at both the local and state levels to ensure stability, prosperity, and efficient governance.

11. Kautilya's Principle of Diplomacy.

In Kautilya's Arthashastra, the principles of diplomacy are integral to statecraft and international relations. Kautilya's approach to diplomacy reflects his pragmatic and strategic mind set, emphasizing flexibility, realpolitik, and the pursuit of state interests. Here's an overview of Kautilya's principles of diplomacy:

1. Realism and Pragmatism

I. Pursuit of SelfInterest: Kautilya's diplomacy is grounded in the pursuit of the state's selfinterest. The primary goal is to enhance the state's power, security, and influence, even if it means employing unconventional or morally ambiguous tactics.

II. Adaptability: Diplomacy should be adaptable to changing circumstances. Kautilya advises rulers to be flexible and pragmatic, adjusting their strategies based on the evolving political landscape and the behaviour of other states.

2. Use of Alliances and Treaties

I. Strategic Alliances: Forming alliances with other states is a key diplomatic strategy. Kautilya recommends forging alliances to strengthen the state's position, gain support in conflicts, and counterbalance rival powers. These alliances should be based on mutual interests and benefits.

II. Treaties and Agreements: Treaties and agreements are tools for securing advantages and ensuring stability. Kautilya emphasizes the importance of carefully negotiating and drafting treaties to protect the state's interests and avoid unfavourable terms.

3. Diplomacy of Deception

I. Strategic Deception: Kautilya advocates for the use of deception as a diplomatic tool. This includes misleading opponents, feigning weakness, or using misinformation to gain a strategic advantage. The objective is to outmanoeuvre rivals and achieve favourable outcomes.

II. Diplomatic Subterfuge: Subterfuge, such as covert operations and espionage, is used to gather intelligence and manipulate rival states. Kautilya views these tactics as essential for gaining insights into the intentions and capabilities of other states.

4. Balance of Power

I.   Power Dynamics: Kautilya's diplomacy involves understanding and manipulating the balance of power among states. By shifting alliances and leveraging geopolitical dynamics, the state can enhance its own position and prevent any single rival from becoming too dominant.

II.   Strategic Positioning: Maintaining a favourable balance of power requires careful positioning and strategy. Kautilya advises rulers to assess the strengths and weaknesses of neighbouring states and adjust their diplomatic approach accordingly.

5. Diplomacy and Warfare

I.   War as a Tool: Diplomacy and warfare are closely intertwined in Kautilya's framework. Diplomacy is used to prepare for or prevent war, and war itself is a means to achieve diplomatic goals. The decision to go to war should be based on strategic calculations and the potential benefits.

II.   War Diplomacy: During conflicts, diplomatic efforts continue to play a role. Negotiations, alliances, and peace treaties are part of the broader strategy to achieve the desired outcomes of war and secure favourable terms.

6. Use of Envoys and Spies

I.   Diplomatic Envoys: Envoys are used to represent the state's interests and negotiate with other states. Kautilya emphasizes the selection of competent and skilled envoys who can effectively carry out diplomatic missions and achieve the state's objectives.

II.   Spies and Intelligence: Espionage is a crucial component of diplomacy. Spies gather information about rival states, their intentions, and their capabilities. This intelligence is used to inform diplomatic strategies and decisions.

7. Diplomacy of Dissuasion

I.   Deterrence: Diplomacy can also involve dissuading other states from pursuing hostile actions. Kautilya suggests using threats, demonstrations of strength, and diplomatic pressure to deter potential aggressors and maintain peace.

II. Strategic Communications: Effective communication is used to convey the state's intentions and capabilities, thereby influencing the behavior of other states and preventing misunderstandings or conflicts.

8. Ethical and Moral Considerations

I. Pragmatic Ethics: While Kautilya's approach to diplomacy is pragmatic and sometimes ruthless, it also acknowledges the importance of maintaining a balance between strategic interests and ethical considerations. The primary focus remains on achieving the state's goals while navigating the complexities of international relations.

Conclusion: In the Arthashastra, Kautilya's principles of diplomacy reflect a strategic and pragmatic approach to statecraft. The emphasis on realism, adaptability, and the pursuit of self-interest underscores the importance of flexibility and strategic thinking in international relations. By leveraging alliances, employing deception, and balancing power, Kautilya's diplomacy aims to enhance the state's position and achieve its objectives in a competitive and complex global environment.

12. Kautilya's Strategies of Diplomacy.

Kautilya's Arthashastra outlines several strategic approaches to diplomacy, focusing on pragmatic and flexible methods to achieve state objectives. These strategies reflect Kautilya's realpolitik perspective and his emphasis on the practicalities of statecraft. Here's a detailed look at Kautilya's strategies of diplomacy:

1. Sandhi (Negotiation and Alliance)

I.   Diplomatic Negotiation: Sandhi involves negotiating treaties and alliances with other states. Kautilya recommends entering into agreements that serve the state's interests, enhance security, and provide strategic advantages.

II. Forming Alliances: Building alliances with other states can help strengthen the state's position, provide support in conflicts, and counterbalance rivals. Alliances should be based on mutual benefit and clear objectives.

2. Vigraha (Conflict and War)

I.   Strategic Warfare: When diplomacy fails or when war is advantageous, Kautilya advises using warfare as a tool to achieve political goals. This includes planning and executing military campaigns to enhance the state's power and achieve strategic objectives.

II. Diplomatic Preparation for War: Before engaging in war, diplomatic efforts should be made to prepare and position the state advantageously. This may involve forming alliances, gathering intelligence, and ensuring that the state is ready for conflict.

3. Asana (Neutrality and Inaction)

I.   Maintaining Neutrality: In certain situations, maintaining a neutral stance can be advantageous. Neutrality allows the state to avoid entanglement in conflicts and preserve its resources while observing the developments in the international arena.

II. Strategic Inaction: Sometimes, refraining from taking immediate action or making premature commitments can be a strategic choice. This allows the state to assess the situation, gather information, and make informed decisions.

4. Yana (Expedition and Expansion)

I. Diplomatic Expeditions: Conducting diplomatic missions and expeditions to other states can help achieve objectives such as forming alliances, negotiating treaties, or gathering intelligence. Envoys and emissaries play a key role in these missions.

II. Expansionist Policies: Kautilya also discusses the strategy of territorial expansion through diplomatic means. This can involve negotiating for additional territory or influencing neighbouring states to align with the state's interests.

5. Danda (Use of Authority and Punishment)

I. Coercive Diplomacy: Danda involves using the state's authority and punitive measures to enforce diplomatic agreements or compel other states to comply with demands. This may include threats of military action or economic sanctions.

II. Enforcement of Agreements: When diplomatic agreements are violated, Kautilya advises using authority and enforcement mechanisms to ensure compliance and protect the state's interests.

6. Sama (Appeasement and Reconciliation)

I. Diplomatic Reconciliation: Sama involves using appeasement and reconciliation strategies to resolve conflicts and build relationships. This can include offering concessions, making compromises, or engaging in dialogue to address grievances.

II. Maintaining Peace: Kautilya emphasizes the importance of maintaining peace and stability through diplomatic efforts. Reconciliation can help prevent conflicts and foster cooperation with other states.

7. Maya (Deception and Manipulation)

I. Diplomatic Deception: Maya involves using deception and manipulation to achieve diplomatic goals. This includes misleading other states about the state's true intentions, capabilities, or plans to gain a strategic advantage.

II. Espionage and Intelligence: Gathering intelligence through espionage is a key aspect of Maya. By understanding the intentions and capabilities of other states, the state can craft more effective diplomatic strategies and responses.

8. Rajadharma (Statecraft and Governance)

I. Principles of Governance: Kautilya integrates diplomatic strategies with principles of effective statecraft and governance. This includes managing internal affairs efficiently, maintaining stability, and ensuring that diplomatic efforts align with overall state objectives.

II. Diplomacy and State Policy: Diplomatic strategies should be aligned with the state's broader policy goals and objectives. Effective governance ensures that diplomatic efforts contribute to the state's long term interests and stability.

9. Strategic Alliances and Rivalries

I. Balancing Rivals: Kautilya advises balancing relationships with rival states by forming alliances with other powers. This helps prevent any single rival from becoming too dominant and enhances the state's strategic position.

II. Opportunistic Alliances: Alliances should be opportunistic and based on current circumstances. Kautilya recommends forming temporary alliances with states that can provide immediate benefits, even if they are not long term partners.

Conclusion: In the Arthashastra, Kautilya's strategies of diplomacy emphasize a pragmatic and strategic approach to statecraft. By employing methods such as negotiation, conflict, neutrality, expansion, coercion, appeasement, deception, and effective governance, Kautilya provides a comprehensive framework for achieving state objectives in a competitive and complex international environment. His focus on flexibility, realpolitik, and strategic thinking reflects a deep understanding of the dynamics of diplomacy and statecraft.

13. Kautilya's Mandala Theory & Kenneth Waltz.

Kautilya's Mandala Theory and Kenneth Waltz's theories in international relations both offer insights into the nature of state behaviour and the dynamics of power, though they originate from different historical and theoretical contexts. Here's a comparative overview of Kautilya's Mandala Theory and Kenneth Waltz's theories:

Kautilya's Mandala Theory-

Mandala Theory, as presented in Kautilya's Arthashastra, describes the geopolitical framework of state relations and how states interact with one another. The term "Mandala" translates to "circle" or "sphere" and reflects the idea of states interacting within a circular model of influence and competition. Key aspects of Mandala Theory include:

1. Geopolitical Configuration

I. Central and Peripheral States: In Mandala Theory, the state is seen as the central power within its own sphere of influence, surrounded by neighbouring states, both friendly and hostile. The central state interacts with these peripheral states based on strategic interests.

II. Dynamic Relationships: The relationships between states are dynamic and can change based on alliances, rivalries, and strategic considerations. The central state constantly adjusts its strategy to maintain or enhance its position within this geopolitical circle.

2. Strategic Interactions

I. Alliances and Rivalries: Kautilya emphasizes the importance of forming alliances and managing rivalries. States must navigate these relationships carefully to maximize their own security and power.

II. Influence and Control: The Mandala Theory suggests that states seek to expand their influence and control over their immediate environment. States use diplomacy, alliances, and, if necessary, military force to achieve their strategic goals.

3. Flexibility and Adaptability

I. Strategic Flexibility: States must be flexible and adaptable, adjusting their strategies based on changing circumstances and the behaviour of other states. This involves shifting alliances, negotiating treaties, and responding to threats.

Kenneth Waltz's Theories-

Kenneth Waltz is known for his contributions to neorealism (or structural realism) in international relations. His theories, particularly those outlined in his seminal work Theory of International Politics (1979), offer a structural perspective on international relations. Key aspects include:

1. Structural Realism

I. Anarchy: Waltz's neorealism posits that the international system is anarchic, meaning there is no overarching authority above states. This creates a self-help system where states must rely on their own capabilities for security and survival.

II. Distribution of Power: Waltz emphasizes the importance of the distribution of power in shaping state behaviour. The balance of power among states influences their actions and interactions within the international system.

2. State Behavior

I. Rational Actors: According to Waltz, states are rational actors seeking to maximize their security and power within the anarchic system. They act based on their perception of threats and opportunities.

II. Security Dilemma: The security dilemma arises when actions taken by a state to increase its security (e.g., military build-up) lead to increased insecurity among other states, potentially resulting in arms races or conflicts.

3. International System

I. Systemic Analysis: Waltz focuses on the structure of the international system rather than the characteristics of individual states. He argues that the system's structure (i.e., the distribution of power) shapes state behaviour and international outcomes.

Comparative Analysis-

1. Theoretical Framework

- Mandala Theory: Focuses on the geopolitical dynamics and strategic interactions between states within a circular framework. It emphasizes the importance of alliances, rivalries, and strategic positioning.
- Waltz's Neorealism: Centres on the anarchic structure of the international system and the distribution of power. It provides a systemic analysis of state behaviour and international relations.

2. Focus on State Behaviour

- Mandala Theory: Offers a more detailed and nuanced view of how states interact based on their immediate geopolitical environment. It highlights the role of strategic alliances and rivalries.
- Waltz's Neorealism: Provides a broader perspective on state behaviour within the international system, focusing on how structural factors like power distribution influence state actions.

3. Flexibility and Adaptability

- Mandala Theory: Emphasizes the need for states to be flexible and adaptable in their strategic interactions. States must continuously adjust their strategies based on the changing dynamics of their geopolitical environment.
- Waltz's Neorealism: While also acknowledging the need for states to respond to their environment, neorealism emphasizes the constraints imposed by the anarchic structure of the international system.

4. Application

- Mandala Theory: Provides insights into the strategies states use to navigate their immediate geopolitical context, including forming alliances and managing rivalries.
- Waltz's Neorealism: Offers a theoretical framework for understanding the broader patterns and structures of international relations, focusing on the systemic factors that shape state behaviour.

Conclusion: Kautilya's Mandala Theory and Kenneth Waltz's neorealism provide complementary perspectives on state behaviour and international relations. Mandala Theory offers a detailed view of strategic interactions within a specific geopolitical context, while Waltz's neorealism provides a systemic analysis of the broader international structure. Both theories highlight the importance of power, strategy, and adaptability in shaping state behaviour and international outcomes.

14. Machiavelli & Kautilya's.

Niccolò Machiavelli and Kautilya (Chanakya) are two influential figures in political philosophy and statecraft, whose works, The Prince and Arthashastra respectively, offer strategic insights into governance and diplomacy. Although they operated in different historical and cultural contexts—Machiavelli in Renaissance Italy and Kautilya in ancient India—there are notable similarities and differences between their ideas.

1. Nature of Power and Statecraft

- Kautilya:

I. Realism: Kautilya's Arthashastra is deeply pragmatic and realist, emphasizing the importance of power, strategic thinking, and the pursuit of state interests.

II. Strategic Statecraft: Kautilya advocates for a multifaceted approach to statecraft, including diplomacy, alliances, espionage, and warfare. He views the ruler as a shrewd strategist who must navigate complex political dynamics to maintain and enhance state power.

- Machiavelli:

I. Political Realism: Machiavelli's The Prince is also grounded in political realism. He advises rulers to be pragmatic, focusing on effective governance and the consolidation of power.

II. Machiavellianism: Machiavelli's approach is often associated with the idea that the ends justify the means. He argues that rulers should be prepared to use deception, manipulation, and cruelty if necessary to maintain their power and achieve political objectives.

2. Role of the Ruler

- Kautilya:

I. Strategic Leader: Kautilya emphasizes the ruler's role as a strategic leader who must be knowledgeable, shrewd, and capable of making difficult decisions. The ruler should use a combination of diplomacy, alliances, and military force to achieve state objectives.

II. Moral Flexibility: While Kautilya acknowledges the importance of moral conduct, he is pragmatic about the need for flexibility in applying ethical principles to achieve political goals.

- Machiavelli:

I. Virtù and Fortuna: Machiavelli introduces the concepts of virtù (the ruler's ability to shape his own destiny) and fortuna (the role of chance or fortune). He argues that a successful ruler must possess virtù to navigate the unpredictable nature of political life.

II. Effective Ruler: Machiavelli advises that the ruler should focus on being effective rather than moral. The ruler must be willing to act immorally if it serves the state's interests and ensures stability.

3. Diplomacy and Alliances

- Kautilya:

I. Mandala Theory: Kautilya's Mandala Theory outlines how states interact within a geopolitical framework, emphasizing the importance of alliances, rivalries, and strategic positioning.

II. Diplomatic Flexibility: Kautilya advocates for forming alliances and managing rivalries based on shifting circumstances. He also recommends the use of deception and intelligence to gain an advantage.

- Machiavelli:

I. Realpolitik: Machiavelli's advice on diplomacy is rooted in realpolitik. He suggests that rulers should form alliances based on pragmatic considerations and be prepared to break them if necessary for the state's advantage.

II. Diplomatic Manoeuvring: Machiavelli also advises rulers to be skilled in diplomacy, using alliances and negotiations to strengthen their position while being wary of the potential for betrayal.

4. Use of Force and Warfare

- Kautilya:

I. Warfare as a Tool: Kautilya views warfare as an integral part of statecraft. He emphasizes strategic planning, intelligence, and the careful use of military force to achieve political goals.

II. Defensive and Offensive Strategies: Kautilya's approach includes both defensive and offensive strategies. He advises rulers on the use of fortifications, military organization, and strategic deployments.

- Machiavelli:

I. Military Preparedness: Machiavelli also recognizes the importance of military strength. He argues that a ruler must maintain a strong and loyal army to defend the state and project power.

II. War and Peace: Machiavelli suggests that rulers should be prepared for war but should seek peace when it benefits the state. He emphasizes the need for military capability as a foundation for effective rule.

5. Ethics and Morality

- Kautilya:

I. Pragmatic Ethics: Kautilya's work is pragmatic regarding ethics. He believes that moral principles should be applied flexibly, depending on the context and the needs of the state.

II. Moral Ambiguity: While ethical conduct is important, Kautilya acknowledges that sometimes it is necessary to act immorally to achieve the state's objectives.

- Machiavelli:

I. Ethical Flexibility: Machiavelli's The Prince is often interpreted as advocating for a flexible approach to ethics. He argues that rulers should prioritize effectiveness over morality and be prepared to use unethical means if they serve the state's interests.

II. Moral Relativism: Machiavelli's work is frequently seen as endorsing moral relativism, where traditional ethical norms are subordinated to political necessity and the pursuit of power.

6. Legacy and Influence

- Kautilya:

I.   Historical Influence: Kautilya's Arthashastra has had a lasting impact on Indian political thought and strategy. His ideas on statecraft, governance, and strategy continue to be studied and applied in various contexts.

II.   Strategic Thinking: Kautilya's emphasis on strategy, diplomacy, and realpolitik has influenced both historical and contemporary discussions on political strategy.

- Machiavelli:

I.   Political Philosophy: Machiavelli's The Prince has had a profound influence on Western political philosophy and is often associated with the concept of Machiavellianism, characterized by political cunning and pragmatic, sometimes unscrupulous, tactics.

II.   Modern Realism: Machiavelli's ideas have contributed to the development of modern political realism and theories of statecraft, influencing thinkers and policymakers across different eras.

Conclusion: Both Kautilya and Machiavelli offer pragmatic and strategic perspectives on governance and diplomacy. While Kautilya's Arthashastra provides a comprehensive guide to statecraft with a focus on strategic interactions and realpolitik, Machiavelli's The Prince emphasizes the importance of effective rule and the willingness to employ morally flexible tactics. Despite their different contexts, both thinkers share a realist approach to politics, emphasizing the importance of power, strategy, and adaptability in statecraft.

15. Economic Thought in Ancient India: Basic features.

Economic thought in ancient India, particularly as reflected in texts such as Kautilya's Arthashastra, the Manusmriti, and various other ancient works, provides a rich and complex view of economic principles and practices. Here are some basic features of ancient Indian economic thought:

1. Agriculture and Land Revenue

- Agricultural Focus:
I. Central Role: Agriculture was the cornerstone of the ancient Indian economy. Land was considered the primary source of wealth, and agricultural production was crucial for sustaining the population and the state.
II. Land Revenue System: Land revenue was a major source of state income. The Arthashastra outlines various methods for assessing and collecting land taxes. Revenue was often based on a portion of the agricultural output, with different rates applied depending on the fertility of the land and the nature of the crops.
- Land Ownership:
I. Private and State Ownership: Land could be owned privately, by the state, or by religious institutions. The state often had rights to land revenue and could also redistribute land as needed.

2. Trade and Commerce

- Internal and External Trade:
I. Trade Networks: Ancient India had extensive trade networks, both within the subcontinent and with other regions, including Central Asia, the Middle East, and Southeast Asia. Major trade routes facilitated the exchange of goods and culture.
II. Trade Goods: Key exports included spices, textiles, and gems, while imports often included luxury items and raw materials not available locally.
- Market Regulation:
I. Market Practices: The Arthashastra provides detailed guidelines for market regulation, including the prevention of fraud, ensuring fair trade practices, and regulating prices and weights.

3. Economic Administration

- Role of the State:

I. Economic Regulation: The state played an active role in economic regulation, including setting standards for weights and measures, managing trade and commerce, and overseeing economic activities.

II. Officials and Departments: The administration included officials responsible for various economic functions, such as tax collection, trade regulation, and land management.

- Economic Policies:

I. Monetary Policies: Ancient Indian texts discuss the use of currency and the management of state finances. The Arthashastra addresses issues related to currency standards, coinage, and financial management.

4. Economic Principles

- Economic Philosophy:

I. Wealth and Prosperity: Economic thought emphasized the importance of wealth and prosperity for both individuals and the state. Economic activities were seen as integral to maintaining and enhancing societal wellbeing.

II. Ethics and Economy: Economic principles were often intertwined with ethical considerations. For instance, the Manusmriti outlines moral guidelines related to economic activities, including the duties of different social classes in economic matters.

- Trade and Wealth Creation:

I. Wealth Accumulation: The accumulation of wealth through trade, commerce, and agriculture was encouraged, but it was also balanced with considerations of fairness and ethical behavior in economic transactions.

5. Labour and Employment

- Role of Labour:

I. Economic Contribution: Labour was recognized as a fundamental component of economic activity. Various texts discuss the roles of different types of labour, including agricultural work, artisanal crafts, and trade.

- Social Classes and Occupations:

I.   Varna System: The social structure, including the Varna system, influenced occupational roles and economic functions. Different classes were assigned specific economic roles and duties.

6. Economic Ethics

- Moral Considerations:

I.   Ethical Conduct: Ethical considerations played a role in economic thought. Principles of honesty, fairness, and justice were emphasized in economic transactions, and unethical practices were discouraged.

II.   Charity and Welfare: Texts often discuss the importance of charity and the responsibility of the wealthy to support the less fortunate, reflecting a concern for social welfare.

7. Trade and Economics in Texts

- Ancient Texts:

I.   Arthashastra: Kautilya's Arthashastra is one of the most comprehensive sources on ancient Indian economic thought, covering topics such as trade, taxation, market regulation, and economic strategy.

II.   Manusmriti: The Manusmriti includes economic principles related to duties, ethics, and social responsibilities, reflecting the intersection of economic and moral thought.

Conclusion: Ancient Indian economic thought reflects a sophisticated understanding of economic principles and practices, integrating concepts of agriculture, trade, administration, and ethical considerations. Texts like the Arthashastra and Manusmriti offer insights into how ancient Indian societies managed their economies and balanced economic activities with social and moral values. The emphasis on agriculture, trade regulation, and state involvement highlights the complexity and depth of ancient Indian economic thought.

16. Economic Thought in Ancient India - Economic ideas on Wealth & population.

Economic thought in ancient India, as reflected in various texts like the Arthashastra, the Manusmriti, and other ancient works, provides insights into how wealth and population were understood and managed. Here's an overview of economic ideas related to wealth and population in ancient India:

1. Wealth

- Concept of Wealth:

I. Wealth as Prosperity: In ancient Indian economic thought, wealth was seen as a key factor in prosperity and the wellbeing of individuals and the state. Wealth included both material assets like land, goods, and money, and nonmaterial assets such as prestige and social status.

II. Sources of Wealth: Wealth was primarily derived from agriculture, trade, and industry. The Arthashastra discusses various sources of wealth, including land revenue, trade profits, and the collection of taxes.

- Accumulation and Management:

I. Agricultural Wealth: Agriculture was the primary source of wealth, and land was considered a critical asset. The management of agricultural resources and the collection of land revenue were central to maintaining and increasing wealth.

II. Trade and Commerce: Trade played a significant role in wealth accumulation. Ancient India engaged in extensive trade with other regions, exporting goods such as spices, textiles, and gems, and importing luxury items and raw materials.

- Economic Policies:

I. Taxation: Effective taxation policies were crucial for wealth management. The Arthashastra outlines methods for assessing and collecting taxes, including land revenue and trade taxes, to ensure a steady flow of state income.

II. Wealth Distribution: The management of wealth also involved policies on wealth distribution. Texts like the Manusmriti suggest principles for fair distribution and the responsibilities of different social classes regarding wealth.

- Ethics of Wealth:

I. Moral Considerations: Economic thought included ethical considerations about wealth. The accumulation of wealth was encouraged, but it was also emphasized that it should be pursued with integrity and fairness. The wealthy were expected to contribute to social welfare and support the less fortunate.

2. Population

- Population and Economic Activity:
I. Role in Economy: The population was seen as both a resource and a responsibility. A larger population provided a labour force for agriculture, trade, and industry, contributing to economic activity and wealth creation.
II. Population Growth: The management of population growth was linked to economic stability. Large populations could lead to increased demand for resources and services, impacting economic planning and state policies.
- Management and Policy:
I. Economic Planning: Ancient texts discuss policies related to population management, including the organization of labour and the allocation of resources. The state was responsible for ensuring that the population's needs were met and that economic activities were effectively managed.
II. Urban and Rural Distribution: Economic thought addressed the distribution of population between urban and rural areas. Urban centers were hubs of trade and administration, while rural areas were primarily agricultural.
- Social Structure and Labour:
I. Varna System: The social structure, including the Varna system, influenced labour allocation and economic roles. Different social classes had specific economic responsibilities, which affected the overall management of the population and resources.
II. Labour Force: The availability and organization of labour were crucial for economic activities. Texts like the Arthashastra provide guidelines on managing labour, including the recruitment and organization of workers for various economic tasks.
- Economic Impact of Population:

I. Demand and Supply: The size of the population influenced demand for goods and services. Economic policies aimed to balance supply with demand, ensuring that resources were used efficiently to support a growing population.

II. Social Welfare: Population management included aspects of social welfare. Ancient texts emphasized the importance of caring for the needy and ensuring that the basic needs of the population were met.

Conclusion: Ancient Indian economic thought reflects a sophisticated understanding of the relationship between wealth and population. Wealth was seen as essential for prosperity and was derived from agriculture, trade, and industry. Effective management of wealth involved taxation, fair distribution, and ethical considerations. Population was viewed as a vital resource, and its management was linked to economic stability and planning. Texts like the Arthashastra and the Manusmriti provide valuable insights into how ancient Indian societies approached these economic concepts, balancing wealth accumulation with ethical considerations and addressing the challenges of managing a growing population.

17. Economic Thought in Ancient India -Land & Agriculture.

Economic thought in ancient India, particularly as articulated in texts like Kautilya's Arthashastra, the Manusmriti, and various other ancient works, provides a comprehensive view of land and agriculture. These aspects were central to the economy and governance of ancient Indian societies. Here's an overview of how land and agriculture were perceived and managed:

1. Land

- Ownership and Control:

I. Types of Land Ownership: Land could be owned privately by individuals, held by the state, or controlled by religious institutions. Ownership rights and responsibilities were well-defined, with the state having significant control over land revenue.

II. State Authority: The state played a crucial role in land management, including the assessment of land for taxation and the redistribution of land as needed. Land grants and redistribution were also used to reward loyal subjects and support religious institutions.

- Land Revenue System:

I. Taxation: Land revenue was a major source of income for the state. The Arthashastra provides detailed methods for assessing and collecting land taxes, often based on a portion of the agricultural output. Different rates were applied depending on factors like land fertility and crop type.

II. Revenue Collection: The process of land revenue collection was systematic, involving periodic assessments and the use of officials to ensure proper collection. The system aimed to balance the needs of the state with the capabilities of the landholders.

- Land Use and Regulation:

I. Land Use Policies: Policies were in place to regulate land use, including the management of agricultural practices and the prevention of land degradation. The Arthashastra discusses the importance of maintaining soil fertility and managing irrigation.

II. Land Reform: The state occasionally engaged in land reform to address issues of land ownership and distribution. Reforms aimed to improve agricultural productivity and ensure fair distribution of land.

2. Agriculture

- Significance of Agriculture:

I. Economic Foundation: Agriculture was the backbone of the ancient Indian economy, providing food, raw materials, and a substantial portion of state revenue. It was central to both daily life and economic planning.

II. Agricultural Practices: Ancient texts describe various agricultural practices, including crop cultivation, irrigation techniques, and soil management. Techniques such as crop rotation and the use of fertilizers were practiced to enhance productivity.

- Crop Cultivation:

I. Types of Crops: Major crops included rice, wheat, barley, pulses, and various fruits and vegetables. The choice of crops depended on regional climate, soil conditions, and market demand.

II. Irrigation: Irrigation was crucial for agriculture, especially in regions with irregular rainfall. Ancient Indian texts discuss the construction and maintenance of irrigation systems, including wells, canals, and tanks.

- Agricultural Labour:

I. Labour Allocation: Labour was organized according to the needs of agricultural activities. This included the use of manual labour for planting, tending, and harvesting crops.

II. Social Structure: The Varna system influenced labour allocation, with different social classes contributing to agricultural work in various capacities. The role of labourers and landowners was well-defined.

- Economic Management:

I. Storage and Distribution: Proper storage and distribution of agricultural produce were essential to prevent waste and ensure food security. Ancient texts provide guidelines on managing granaries and distributing surplus produce.

II. Market Regulation: Markets played a role in the distribution of agricultural goods. The Arthashastra includes provisions for regulating market prices, preventing fraud, and ensuring fair trade practices.

- Agricultural Policies:

I.   Support and Incentives: The state implemented policies to support agriculture, such as providing subsidies, offering loans to farmers, and investing in infrastructure like irrigation systems.

II. Disaster Management: Policies were also in place to address issues related to crop failure and natural disasters. Relief measures and assistance were provided to affected farmers.

3. Challenges and Solutions

- Challenges:

I.   Resource Management: Managing land and agricultural resources effectively was a significant challenge, given the variability in soil fertility, water availability, and climatic conditions.

II. Population Pressure: Increasing population pressure could strain agricultural resources and lead to challenges in food production and distribution.

- Solutions:

I.   Innovative Practices: The development and adoption of innovative agricultural practices, such as improved irrigation techniques and crop management strategies, helped address challenges and enhance productivity.

II. State Intervention: The state played an active role in addressing agricultural issues, including implementing policies to support farmers, manage land resources, and ensure food security.

Conclusion: Economic thought in ancient India reflected a sophisticated understanding of land and agriculture. Land was central to the economy, with well-defined ownership rights and a systematic approach to revenue collection. Agriculture was the foundation of economic activity, with a focus on effective land use, crop cultivation, and labour management. Ancient texts like the Arthashastra and the Manusmriti provide valuable insights into how ancient Indian societies managed their agricultural resources and addressed the challenges of land and agriculture. The integration of state policies, innovative practices, and ethical considerations underscores the complexity and depth of ancient Indian economic thought.

18. Economic Thought in Ancient India -Animal Husbandry.

Animal husbandry in ancient India was an important aspect of economic thought and practice, reflecting its role in agriculture, trade, and daily life. Ancient Indian texts and historical records provide insights into how animal husbandry was managed, the types of animals involved, and the economic implications. Here's an overview of the economic thought related to animal husbandry in ancient India:

1. Importance of Animal Husbandry

- Economic Contribution:
  I. Agricultural Support: Animals played a crucial role in agriculture. They were used for plowing fields, transporting goods, and providing manure, which was essential for soil fertility.
  II. Product Supply: Animal husbandry provided a variety of products, including milk, meat, leather, and wool. These products were important for both subsistence and trade.
- Daily Life and Livelihood:
  I. Rural Economy: In rural areas, animal husbandry was a key component of the economy. Families and communities relied on animals for their livelihood, including farming, transportation, and consumption.

2. Types of Animals

- Cattle:
  I. Primary Livestock: Cattle were the most important animals in ancient India. They were used for ploughing, carrying loads, and as a source of milk and manure.
  II. Sacred Status: Cattle, especially cows, held a sacred status in many regions of ancient India, reflecting their importance in both economic and cultural contexts.
- Elephants:
  I. Royal and Religious Uses: Elephants were highly valued for their use in warfare, royal processions, and religious ceremonies. They were also used for heavy labour and transportation.
  II. Economic Value: Elephants were considered a sign of wealth and power, and their upkeep involved significant resources.

- Horses:

I. Military and Trade: Horses were crucial for military purposes, including cavalry units. They were also used for transportation and trade.

II. Trade and Exchange: Horse trade was significant, with horses being imported and exported as part of regional and international trade networks.

- Other Livestock:

I. Goats and Sheep: Goats and sheep were raised for their milk, meat, and wool. They were particularly important in regions where cattle might not be as practical.

II. Poultry: Chickens and ducks were kept for their eggs and meat, contributing to dietary diversity.

3. Animal Husbandry Practices

- Breeding and Care:

I. Selective Breeding: Breeding practices aimed to improve the quality and productivity of livestock. Selective breeding was used to enhance traits such as strength, milk production, and disease resistance.

II. Animal Care: Proper care and management of animals were essential for their productivity and health. This included feeding, shelter, and healthcare.

- Feeding and Nutrition:

I. Forage and Supplements: Animals were fed a diet that included forage, grains, and supplements. Manure from animals was used to fertilize crops, creating a cycle of productivity.

- Housing and Infrastructure:

I. Shelters: Animals were provided with shelters to protect them from harsh weather conditions and predators. The design of animal housing varied depending on the type of animal and regional conditions.

4. Economic and Trade Implications

- Trade and Exchange:

I. Animal Products: Animal products, such as milk, meat, leather, and wool, were traded locally and across regions. This trade contributed to the economy and supported various industries.

II. Import and Export: Horses, elephants, and other specialized animals were often traded across regions and empires, reflecting their economic and strategic importance.

- Manure Management:

I. Fertilizer Use: Animal manure was a valuable resource for maintaining soil fertility. It was used to enrich agricultural lands, enhancing crop yields and contributing to sustainable farming practices.

- Economic Value:

I. Wealth and Status: Ownership of large herds of cattle or elephants was a symbol of wealth and status. It reflected the economic and social standing of individuals or families.

5. Cultural and Religious Aspects

- Sacred Animals:

I. Religious Significance: Animals, especially cattle, had religious and cultural significance. They were often associated with deities and religious rituals, influencing their treatment and management.

II. Cultural Practices: Animal husbandry practices were influenced by cultural beliefs and customs, including dietary restrictions and ritual practices.

- Ethical Considerations:

I. Humane Treatment: Ancient texts often discuss the ethical treatment of animals, reflecting a concern for their wellbeing and the importance of humane practices.

Conclusion: Animal husbandry in ancient India was an integral part of the economy and daily life, with significant implications for agriculture, trade, and cultural practices. The management of livestock, including cattle, elephants, and horses, played a crucial role in supporting agricultural productivity, military capabilities, and trade. Ancient texts and historical records provide valuable insights into the practices and economic thought related to animal husbandry, highlighting its importance in the socioeconomic and cultural fabric of ancient Indian societies.

19. Economic Thought in Ancient India –Labour.

In ancient India, labour was a critical component of the economy, deeply intertwined with social structures, agricultural practices, and economic management. Economic thought regarding labour in ancient India reflects a nuanced understanding of its role in productivity, societal organization, and economic policy. Here's an overview of the key aspects related to labour in ancient Indian economic thought:

1. Role of Labour

- Economic Contribution:

I. Agriculture: Labour was essential for agricultural activities, including planting, tending, and harvesting crops. Since agriculture was the backbone of the ancient Indian economy, the organization and management of labour were crucial for productivity.

II. Craftsmanship and Industry: Labour also contributed to various industries, such as weaving, metallurgy, and pottery. Artisans and craftsmen played a significant role in producing goods for both local consumption and trade.

- Daily Life and Livelihood:

I. Subsistence and Trade: Labour was fundamental to daily life and subsistence. In rural areas, families and communities relied on manual labour for farming, while in urban areas, labour contributed to trade and artisanal activities.

II. Economic Activity: The division of labour and specialization were key aspects of economic activity, with different roles assigned based on skills, social status, and economic needs.

2. Types of Labour

- Agricultural Labour:

I. Manual Labour: Manual labour was central to farming activities. This included tasks such as plowing, sowing, weeding, and harvesting. Labourers worked in fields and were crucial for maintaining agricultural productivity.

II. Seasonal Work: Agricultural labour often followed seasonal patterns, with peak periods of work during planting and harvest times.

- Artisanal and Craft Labour:

I. Specialized Skills: Skilled artisans and craftsmen engaged in activities like weaving, metalworking, and pottery. Their labour was important for creating goods that supported both local economies and trade.

II. Trade Goods: Artisanal products were traded locally and regionally, contributing to economic exchange and the development of trade networks.

- Service and Domestic Labour:

I. Household Work: Domestic labour included tasks such as cooking, cleaning, and maintaining household goods. This labour was often performed by women and was essential for daily life.

II. Personal Services: In urban centres, various personal services, including those provided by barbers, teachers, and entertainers, contributed to the economy.

3. Labour Organization and Management

- Social Structure:

I. Varna System: The Varna system influenced labour organization, with different social classes assigned specific economic roles and responsibilities. This system impacted how labour was allocated and managed within society.

II. Guilds and Associations: In urban areas, artisans and merchants often formed guilds or associations to organize their labour, set standards, and regulate trade practices.

- Labour Contracts and Compensation:

I. Wages and Payments: Labourers were typically compensated with wages, which could be in the form of cash, goods, or other benefits. The compensation varied based on the type of labour, the region, and the prevailing economic conditions.

II. Contractual Agreements: Labour contracts and agreements were used to formalize relationships between employers and workers. These agreements outlined the terms of work, payment, and other conditions.

- Management Practices:

I. Supervision and Coordination: Effective management of labour required supervision and coordination, particularly in large scale agricultural or construction projects. This included organizing labour forces and ensuring productivity.

II. Training and Skill Development: Training and skill development were important for enhancing labour efficiency and productivity. This included apprenticeship systems for artisans and specialized training for agricultural techniques.

4. Economic and Social Implications

- Productivity and Growth:

I. Economic Output: Efficient use of labour was crucial for economic productivity and growth. Labour management practices aimed to maximize output and ensure the sustainability of economic activities.

II. Technological Advancements: Advances in agricultural techniques and tools, influenced by labour practices, contributed to increased productivity and economic development.

- Social Dynamics:

I. Class and Status: Labour roles were often linked to social class and status. The division of labour reflected societal hierarchies and the allocation of economic roles based on social position.

II. Economic Inequality: Labour practices and compensation could also reflect economic inequality, with differences in wages and working conditions based on social status and occupation.

- Ethical Considerations:

I. Fair Treatment: Ethical considerations regarding labour included concerns about fair treatment and humane working conditions. Ancient texts sometimes addressed the responsibilities of employers and the rights of workers.

II. Support for the Needy: Economic thought included provisions for supporting those unable to work due to age, illness, or other factors. Social welfare practices aimed to address the needs of the vulnerable.

5. Economic Thought and Labour Policy

- State Policies:

I. Regulation and Oversight: The state played a role in regulating labour practices and ensuring fair treatment. This included overseeing labour contracts, setting standards, and addressing disputes.

II.   Support for Labour: Policies aimed to support labour through various means, including infrastructure development, training programs, and incentives for productivity.

- Economic Strategy:

I.   Labour and Economic Planning: Labour considerations were integral to economic planning and strategy. Effective labour management was essential for achieving economic goals and ensuring sustainable development.

Conclusion: Economic thought in ancient India reflected a sophisticated understanding of labour and its role in the economy. Labour was essential for agriculture, industry, and daily life, with its organization and management influenced by social structures and economic needs. Ancient Indian texts and historical records provide valuable insights into how labour was perceived, managed, and utilized, highlighting its importance in economic productivity and societal organization. The integration of ethical considerations, social dynamics, and state policies underscores the complexity of labour in ancient Indian economic thought.

20. Economic Thought in Ancient India -Wage & Social securities.

Economic thought in ancient India regarding wages and social security's reflects a sophisticated understanding of labour relations, compensation, and social welfare. These aspects were crucial for ensuring economic stability and social cohesion. Here's an overview of how wages and social securities were perceived and managed in ancient Indian economic thought:

1. Wages

- Forms of Compensation:
  I. Monetary Wages: Wages could be paid in the form of money, though the use of coinage was more prevalent in urban areas and among higher classes. In rural areas, wages were often paid in kind, such as with food, goods, or services.
  II. In-kind Payment: For many labourers, especially in agricultural settings, compensation might include a share of the produce or other goods. This form of payment was common in regions where monetary transactions were less practical.

- Types of Labour:
  I. Agricultural Labour: Agricultural workers were compensated based on their role and the scale of the farming operation. Payment could be a fixed wage, a share of the harvest, or a combination of both.
  II. Artisanal and Craft Labour: Skilled artisans and craftsmen often received payment based on the value of their goods or the services they provided. Prices for artisanal products were set by market standards and guild regulations.

- Wage Determination:
  I. Market Rates: Wages were influenced by market rates and the demand for specific types of labour. This included variations based on the region, the skill level of the labourer, and the type of work performed.
  II. Negotiation and Contracts: Wage rates were sometimes negotiated between employers and workers, with formal agreements or contracts specifying the terms of employment and compensation.

- Labour Conditions:

I. Work Hours: While specific details on work hours are less documented, labour conditions generally adhered to seasonal and agricultural cycles, with peak periods requiring more intensive work.

II. Quality and Fairness: Ethical considerations regarding wages included ensuring fair compensation for work performed. Ancient texts sometimes addressed issues related to fair wages and the responsibilities of employers.

2. Social Securities

- Support for the Vulnerable:

I. Social Welfare: Social welfare provisions aimed to support individuals who were unable to work due to age, illness, or other factors. This included support from family, community, or state resources.

II. Charitable Institutions: Religious and charitable institutions often played a role in providing support to the needy. Temples and monasteries sometimes offered food, shelter, and medical care to the poor and elderly.

- Family and Community Support:

I. Family Responsibility: In many cases, family members were responsible for providing support to elderly or ill relatives. The family unit served as a primary source of social security.

II. Community Networks: Communities often had informal networks of support, where members helped each other in times of need, reflecting a communal approach to social welfare.

- State Involvement:

I. Government Programs: While direct state involvement in social security was less formalized compared to modern systems, ancient texts indicate some level of state responsibility for welfare. This included relief measures during times of famine or natural disasters.

II. Public Assistance: The state could provide assistance through infrastructure projects, food distribution, and other forms of support to ensure social stability and economic wellbeing.

- Legal and Ethical Framework:

I. Legal Provisions: Texts like the Manusmriti and the Arthashastra provide guidelines on the responsibilities of employers and the rights of workers. These texts reflect an understanding of fair treatment and ethical considerations in labour relations.

II. Ethical Considerations: Ethical principles guided social securities, emphasizing the importance of compassion, fairness, and support for those in need. This included both moral obligations and practical measures to address social inequalities.

3. Economic and Social Impact

- Economic Stability:

I. Labour Market Efficiency: Effective management of wages and social securities contributed to economic stability by ensuring a productive and motivated workforce. Fair compensation and support mechanisms helped maintain economic balance.

II. Productivity and Growth: Adequate compensation and social support systems contributed to overall economic growth by promoting productivity and reducing social unrest.

- Social Cohesion:

I. Community Welfare: Social security measures and community support helped maintain social cohesion and stability. Providing for the vulnerable and ensuring fair treatment of labour contributed to social harmony.

II. Moral and Ethical Values: Ethical considerations in labour and social securities reflected broader moral values and cultural norms, influencing societal attitudes towards work, compensation, and welfare.

Conclusion: Economic thought in ancient India regarding wages and social security's reflects a nuanced understanding of labour relations, compensation, and social support. Wages were determined by market rates and negotiated agreements, with compensation often provided in kind or through shares of produce. Social securities were addressed through family support, community networks, and, to some extent, state involvement. Ancient Indian texts provide insights into the principles guiding fair treatment and ethical considerations in labour relations. These aspects highlight the complexity and depth of ancient Indian economic thought, emphasizing the importance of fairness, support, and stability in managing labour and social welfare.

21. Economic Thought in Ancient India -Public finance & taxation.

Economic thought in ancient India concerning public finance and taxation reveals a sophisticated understanding of how to manage state resources and ensure economic stability. Ancient texts like Kautilya's Arthashastra, the Manusmriti, and other historical records provide insights into the principles and practices of public finance and taxation in ancient Indian societies. Here's an overview:

1. Public Finance

- Role and Purpose:

I. State Revenue: Public finance in ancient India was primarily concerned with managing the revenue generated from various sources, including taxes, trade, and resources. This revenue was essential for maintaining state functions, such as administration, defence, infrastructure, and public welfare.

II. Economic Management: Effective public finance management aimed to ensure the efficient use of resources, balance budgets, and support economic development and stability.

- Revenue Sources:

I. Land Revenue: Land revenue was the primary source of state income. The Arthashastra details methods for assessing and collecting land taxes based on the productivity and type of land.

II. Trade and Commerce: Revenue was also generated from trade and commerce, including customs duties and taxes on goods and services. Ancient India engaged in extensive trade, contributing significantly to state revenue.

III. Resource Extraction: The extraction of natural resources, such as minerals and forest products, provided additional sources of revenue. The state regulated and taxed these activities to benefit from resource wealth.

- Expenditure:

I. Administrative Costs: Public finance covered the costs of running the administration, including salaries for officials, infrastructure maintenance, and other administrative expenses.

II. Defence and Security: Expenditure on defence and security was crucial for maintaining the state's sovereignty and stability. This included funding for the military, fortifications, and security measures.

III. Public Works: Investment in public works, such as roads, irrigation systems, and urban infrastructure, was essential for economic development and the welfare of the population.

- Budgeting and Planning:

I. Financial Planning: The state engaged in financial planning to manage revenues and expenditures effectively. This included budgeting for various state activities and ensuring financial stability.

II. Resource Allocation: Allocating resources efficiently was key to achieving economic and administrative goals. The state prioritized spending based on needs and strategic objectives.

2. Taxation

- Principles of Taxation:

I. Fairness and Equity: Taxation principles aimed to ensure fairness and equity. Taxes were often based on the ability to pay, with considerations for the economic capacity of individuals and regions.

II. Efficiency: Taxation practices sought to be efficient and minimize administrative costs. The goal was to collect taxes in a manner that was practical and did not hinder economic activity.

- Types of Taxes:

I. Land Tax: The primary form of taxation, land tax was assessed based on the land's productivity and potential output. The Arthashastra provides detailed methods for assessing land value and collecting revenue.

II. Trade Taxes: Taxes were imposed on trade and commerce, including customs duties on imports and exports. These taxes contributed to state revenue and regulated economic activity.

III. Excise Taxes: Excise taxes were levied on specific goods and services, such as alcoholic beverages and luxury items. These taxes helped regulate consumption and generate additional revenue.

- Tax Collection:

I. Administrative Mechanisms: The collection of taxes was managed by state officials, who were responsible for assessing, collecting, and ensuring compliance. The Arthashastra outlines the roles and responsibilities of tax collectors and officials.

II. Enforcement and Compliance: Ensuring compliance with tax regulations was crucial for maintaining revenue. The state implemented measures to enforce tax laws and address evasion or disputes.

- Tax Relief and Exemptions:

I. Special Provisions: The state sometimes provided tax relief or exemptions in specific circumstances, such as during times of natural disaster or for certain social classes or religious institutions.

II. Support for Agriculture: Tax relief for farmers and agricultural producers was occasionally provided to support agricultural activities and ensure food security.

3. Economic and Social Impact

- Economic Stability:

I. Revenue and Expenditure Balance: Managing public finance and taxation effectively contributed to economic stability. Ensuring a balance between revenue and expenditure was crucial for preventing deficits and maintaining financial health.

II. Investment in Infrastructure: Investment in infrastructure through public finance supported economic development and improved the quality of life for citizens.

- Social Welfare:

I. Public Services: Revenue from taxation supported public services, including education, healthcare, and social welfare programs. These services contributed to the wellbeing of the population.

II. Social Cohesion: Fair and effective taxation helped maintain social cohesion by ensuring that the burden of taxation was distributed equitably and that state resources were used for the common good.

- Administrative Efficiency:

I. Government Functioning: Efficient public finance management supported the smooth functioning of the government. It enabled the state to fulfil its administrative and governance responsibilities effectively.

Conclusion: Economic thought in ancient India regarding public finance and taxation reflects a well-developed understanding of managing state resources, ensuring economic stability, and supporting societal needs. Public finance encompassed revenue generation, expenditure management, and budgeting, while taxation principles aimed to balance fairness, efficiency, and economic impact. Ancient texts like the Arthashastra provide valuable insights into the practices and principles guiding public finance and taxation in ancient Indian societies, highlighting their importance in maintaining state functions, promoting economic development, and supporting social welfare.

22. Economic Thought in Ancient India -Pricing & price control.

Economic thought in ancient India regarding pricing and price control reveals an intricate understanding of market dynamics, economic regulation, and the role of state intervention in ensuring fairness and stability. Ancient texts and historical practices provide insights into how pricing was managed and controlled in various economic contexts. Here's an overview:

1. Pricing Mechanisms

- Market Pricing:

I. Supply and Demand: Pricing in ancient India was influenced by basic economic principles of supply and demand. Prices for goods and services fluctuated based on availability, demand, and market conditions.

II. Marketplaces: Urban centres and marketplaces were crucial for setting prices. Merchants and traders engaged in negotiations and transactions, reflecting market driven pricing.

- Standardized Pricing:

I. Trade Goods: For certain goods, especially those of significant economic or strategic importance, standardized pricing mechanisms were sometimes used. This helped maintain consistency and fairness in trade.

II. Regulated Prices: In some cases, prices were regulated by the state to prevent excessive inflation or exploitation. This included setting maximum prices for essential goods.

2. Price Control

- State Intervention:

I. Regulatory Measures: The state occasionally intervened in pricing to control inflation, prevent hoarding, and ensure the availability of essential goods. This was particularly important during times of scarcity or economic crisis.

II. Price Fixing: The state sometimes fixed prices for staple goods and commodities to prevent price gouging and protect consumers. For example, the price of grains and other essential items could be regulated to ensure affordability.

- Economic Texts and Guidelines:

I. Arthashastra: Kautilya's Arthashastra provides detailed guidelines on price control and market regulation. It includes principles for setting fair prices, monitoring markets, and addressing issues like price manipulation and market distortions.

II. Price Surveillance: The Arthashastra emphasizes the importance of monitoring markets and ensuring that prices remain fair. It details the roles of officials and agents in overseeing market transactions and enforcing pricing regulations.

- Market Regulation:

I. Quality Control: Ensuring the quality of goods was also a part of price control. The state regulated the quality of products to prevent substandard goods from being sold at high prices.

II. Weights and Measures: Accurate weights and measures were crucial for fair pricing. The state established standards and regulations to ensure that goods were sold in the correct quantities and measurements.

3. Pricing for Public Welfare

- Essential Goods:

I. Subsidies and Relief: The state sometimes provided subsidies or relief for essential goods to ensure they were accessible to all segments of society, especially during times of scarcity or economic hardship.

II. Support for Farmers: Pricing policies often included provisions for supporting farmers by ensuring fair prices for their produce and protecting them from exploitation by middlemen.

- Fair Trade Practices:

I. Market Fairness: Ensuring fair trade practices was important for maintaining trust and stability in markets. This included regulating prices to prevent unfair practices and ensuring equitable access to goods.

II. Consumer Protection: The state's role in price control also involved protecting consumers from unfair pricing practices and ensuring that markets functioned efficiently and transparently.

4. Economic and Social Impact

- Economic Stability:

I. Price Stability: Effective price control and regulation contributed to economic stability by preventing extreme fluctuations in prices and ensuring a steady supply of essential goods.

II. Market Efficiency: Proper regulation helped maintain market efficiency by preventing monopolistic practices and promoting healthy competition.

- Social Welfare:

I. Access to Essentials: By controlling prices of essential goods and providing subsidies or relief, the state ensured that all citizens had access to necessary items, contributing to overall social welfare.

II. Economic Equity: Price control measures helped reduce economic disparities by preventing exploitation and ensuring fair pricing for both consumers and producers.

- Administrative Efficiency:

I. Regulatory Oversight: Effective price control required efficient administrative oversight and enforcement. This included monitoring markets, setting regulations, and addressing any issues related to pricing and market practices.

5. Challenges and Limitations

I. Implementation Issues: Implementing price control measures could be challenging, particularly in large and diverse economies. Ensuring compliance and dealing with market disruptions required careful management.

II. Resistance: There could be resistance from traders and merchants who were affected by price controls. Balancing regulatory measures with market needs was essential for maintaining stability.

Conclusion: Economic thought in ancient India concerning pricing and price control reflects a nuanced understanding of market dynamics, state intervention, and the role of regulation in maintaining economic stability and fairness. Ancient texts like the Arthashastra provide valuable insights into the principles and practices of pricing and market regulation, highlighting the importance of fair pricing, quality control, and administrative oversight. Effective management of pricing and price control contributed to economic stability, social welfare, and the efficient functioning of markets in ancient Indian societies.

23. Economic Thought in Ancient India –Trade.

Trade was a vital component of the ancient Indian economy, playing a crucial role in its development and interaction with other regions. Economic thought regarding trade in ancient India reflects a sophisticated understanding of market dynamics, trade practices, and economic policies. Here's an overview of key aspects related to trade in ancient Indian economic thought:

1. Trade Networks and Routes

- Internal Trade:
  I. Regional Markets: Ancient India had a well-developed network of regional markets and trade routes. Major urban centres and trading towns facilitated the exchange of goods within the subcontinent.
  II. Agricultural Produce: Internal trade often involved the exchange of agricultural produce, handicrafts, and other goods between rural areas and urban centres.

- External Trade:
  I. Trade Routes: India was connected to other regions through several major trade routes. Key routes included the Silk Road, which linked India with Central Asia and China, and maritime routes connecting India with the Middle East, Southeast Asia, and Africa.
  II. Maritime Trade: India's extensive coastline enabled maritime trade with distant regions. Ports such as Alexandria, Muziris, and Bharukaccha were significant hubs for trade across the Indian Ocean.

- Trade Partners:
  I. Central Asia and China: India traded with Central Asian and Chinese regions, exchanging goods such as silk, spices, and textiles.
  II. Middle East and Africa: Trade with the Middle East and Africa included the exchange of spices, precious stones, and textiles. Indian merchants also engaged in trade with regions like the Roman Empire and the Arabian Peninsula.

2. Trade Goods

- Exports:
  I. Spices: India was renowned for its spices, including black pepper, cardamom, and cinnamon. Spices were highly valued and in demand across the ancient world.

II.   Textiles: Indian textiles, such as silk, cotton, and woollen fabrics, were widely traded. Indian cloths and garments were sought after for their quality and craftsmanship.

III.   Jewellery and Gems: Precious stones and Jewellery, including diamonds, rubies, and emeralds, were significant exports from India.

- Imports:

I.   Metals and Minerals: India imported metals such as gold, silver, and copper from other regions. These were used for currency, Jewellery, and other purposes.

II.   Luxury Goods: Luxury items, including fine textiles and exotic goods, were imported to meet the demands of the elite and wealthy classes in ancient Indian society.

3. Trade Practices and Regulation

- Commercial Activities:

I.   Merchant Guilds: Merchant guilds played a crucial role in regulating trade practices. They set standards for quality, negotiated trade agreements, and managed trade routes.

II.   Marketplaces: Urban marketplaces and trade centres were hubs for commercial activity. Traders conducted transactions, negotiated prices, and engaged in trade both domestically and internationally.

- Regulation and Taxation:

I.   Customs Duties: The state imposed customs duties on trade goods to regulate commerce and generate revenue. Duties were collected at key trade centres and ports.

II.   Trade Laws: Ancient texts, such as the Arthashastra, provide insights into trade laws and regulations. These laws governed trade practices, dispute resolution, and the protection of traders' rights.

- Currency and Exchange:

I.   Coins and Barter: Trade transactions were conducted using coins made of various metals. In addition to coinage, barter systems were used in some transactions, especially in local or less formal trade.

4. Economic Impact of Trade

- Economic Growth:

I. Wealth and Prosperity: Trade contributed to the wealth and prosperity of ancient Indian states and cities. The influx of revenue from trade supported economic development and state functions.

II. Cultural Exchange: Trade facilitated cultural exchange and the spread of ideas, technologies, and cultural practices between India and other regions.

- Urban Development:

I. Growth of Cities: Trade led to the growth of urban centres and commercial hubs. Cities such as Pataliputra, Taxila, and Ujjain became major trade centres with thriving economies.

- Regional Specialization:

I. Specialized Production: Trade encouraged regional specialization, with different areas focusing on producing specific goods for export. This specialization contributed to efficiency and economic development.

5. Challenges and Risks

- Market Fluctuations:

I. Price Variability: Trade involved fluctuations in prices due to changes in supply and demand. Price volatility could impact both traders and consumers.

II. Economic Instability: External factors, such as political instability or changes in trade routes, could affect trade and economic stability.

- Logistical Challenges:

I. Transportation: Transporting goods over long distances involved logistical challenges, including managing caravan routes and maritime navigation.

II. Security: Ensuring the safety of trade routes and protecting merchants from theft and piracy were essential for maintaining trade.

6. Historical Sources and Texts

- Arthashastra:

I. Economic Treatise: Kautilya's Arthashastra provides detailed information on trade practices, including regulations, taxation, and the management of trade routes. It reflects the strategic importance of trade in ancient Indian economic thought.

- Jain and Buddhist Texts:

I.   Historical Records: Jain and Buddhist texts offer insights into trade practices, including descriptions of trade routes, goods traded, and the role of merchants in ancient Indian society.

Conclusion: Economic thought in ancient India regarding trade reflects a deep understanding of market dynamics, trade practices, and the role of regulation in facilitating commerce. Trade was crucial for economic growth, cultural exchange, and urban development, with a well-established network of internal and external trade routes. The management of trade, including practices related to regulation, taxation, and currency, was integral to maintaining economic stability and prosperity. Ancient texts like the Arthashastra provide valuable insights into the complexities of trade in ancient Indian societies, highlighting its significance in shaping economic and social developments.

24. Economic Thought in Ancient India –Distribution.

Economic thought in ancient India regarding distribution involves understanding how goods and resources were allocated among different segments of society. This distribution was influenced by various factors, including social structures, economic policies, and market mechanisms. Here's an overview of distribution practices and ideas in ancient Indian economic thought:

1. Principles of Distribution

- Equity and Fairness:
  I. Social Hierarchies: Distribution was often influenced by social hierarchies and caste systems. Higher castes and classes typically had greater access to resources and wealth, while lower castes faced more restrictions.
  II. Ethical Considerations: Ancient texts, including the Arthashastra and the Manusmriti, reflect ethical considerations in distribution, emphasizing fairness and the welfare of society. There were guidelines for equitable distribution of resources, especially in times of scarcity.

- Market Mechanisms:
  I. Supply and Demand: Distribution was influenced by market mechanisms where supply and demand determined the allocation of goods and services. Prices, availability, and trade practices affected how resources were distributed.
  II. Regional Distribution: Different regions had varying access to resources, which influenced the distribution of goods across the subcontinent. Trade and transportation played key roles in redistributing goods from surplus areas to those with shortages.

2. Methods of Distribution

- Agricultural Produce:
  I. Land Ownership: Distribution of agricultural produce was affected by land ownership and tenancy arrangements. Landowners typically received a larger share of the produce, while tenants and labourers received a portion based on agreements.

II. Grain Storage: Systems for storing and distributing grain were established to manage surplus and scarcity. This included state managed granaries and storage facilities for distributing grain during times of need.

- Goods and Services:

I. Marketplaces: Goods and services were distributed through marketplaces, where traders and merchants sold their products. Marketplaces served as hubs for the exchange and distribution of goods.

II. Guilds and Associations: Merchant guilds and craft associations played a role in organizing and regulating the distribution of goods. They set standards for quality, managed trade routes, and ensured fair practices.

- State and Temple Contributions:

I. Public Distribution: The state sometimes intervened in distribution, especially during times of crisis. This included providing relief and distributing essential goods to affected populations.

II. Temple Contributions: Temples and religious institutions also played a role in distribution, providing food, shelter, and resources to the needy. This was part of their charitable activities and contributions to social welfare.

3. Distribution of Wealth

- Income and Wealth Distribution:

I. Social Classes: Distribution of wealth was influenced by social classes and economic status. Wealth was concentrated among the elite and ruling classes, while common people and labourers had limited access to resources.

II. Redistribution Mechanisms: Some ancient texts and practices included mechanisms for redistributing wealth, such as charitable giving, state interventions, and support for the poor.

- Taxation and Revenue:

I. Tax Collection: Revenue from taxation was used to fund public projects, administration, and welfare programs. The distribution of tax revenue was crucial for managing state functions and supporting economic activities.

II. Public Works: Investment in public works, such as infrastructure and irrigation projects, helped in the equitable distribution of resources by improving access and efficiency.

4. Social and Economic Impact

- Economic Stability:

I. Resource Allocation: Effective distribution of resources contributed to economic stability by ensuring that goods and services reached various segments of society. This helped in preventing shortages and maintaining market equilibrium.

II. Preventing Scarcity: Systems for managing distribution during times of scarcity helped prevent social unrest and ensured that essential resources were available to all.

- Social Welfare:

I. Support Systems: Distribution practices included provisions for social welfare, such as support for the elderly, poor, and disabled. This was often facilitated by the state, religious institutions, and community networks.

II. Charitable Activities: Charitable activities by temples and affluent individuals played a role in supporting disadvantaged groups and contributing to social cohesion.

- Cultural and Ethical Values:

I. Moral Principles: Distribution practices were guided by moral and ethical principles, reflecting the values of fairness, compassion, and responsibility. Ancient texts often emphasized the importance of equitable distribution and social responsibility.

5. Challenges and Limitations

- Inequality:

I. Social Inequality: Distribution was often influenced by social hierarchies and caste systems, leading to unequal access to resources and wealth. This was a significant challenge in achieving equitable distribution.

II. Economic Disparities: Economic disparities between regions and social classes could impact the fairness of distribution, with wealth and resources concentrated among the elite.

- Administrative Challenges:

I.   Logistical Issues: Managing distribution required effective administrative mechanisms and logistics. Ensuring that resources were distributed efficiently and fairly could be challenging, especially in large and diverse regions.

II.   Corruption and Mismanagement: Instances of corruption and mismanagement could affect the effectiveness of distribution systems, leading to unequal access and inefficiencies.

Conclusion: Economic thought in ancient India regarding distribution reflects a complex interplay of social, economic, and administrative factors. Distribution practices were influenced by market mechanisms, social hierarchies, and ethical principles. The distribution of agricultural produce, goods, and wealth was managed through various methods, including market exchanges, state interventions, and charitable activities. While there were challenges related to inequality and administrative efficiency, the principles guiding distribution aimed to promote fairness, stability, and social welfare. Ancient Indian economic thought provides valuable insights into the management of resources and the role of distribution in maintaining economic and social equilibrium.

25. Economic Thought in Ancient India -Economic functions of state.

In ancient India, the economic functions of the state were crucial for maintaining stability, promoting prosperity, and managing resources effectively. These functions were guided by various texts and practices, reflecting a sophisticated understanding of governance and economic management. Here's an overview of the economic functions of the state in ancient India:

1. Revenue Collection and Taxation

- Revenue Sources:
I. Land Revenue: The primary source of state revenue was land tax, which was assessed based on the productivity and type of land. The Arthashastra outlines methods for evaluating land and collecting taxes.
II. Trade and Commerce: Revenue was also generated from trade and commerce, including customs duties, market taxes, and fees on goods and services.
III. Resource Extraction: The state collected revenue from the extraction of natural resources, such as minerals, forest products, and other resources.
- Taxation Policies:
I. Tax Rates and Assessment: The state set tax rates and assessed taxes based on various criteria, including land productivity and economic capacity. Taxation policies aimed to balance revenue needs with fairness and economic impact.
II. Revenue Management: Effective management of revenue involved budgeting, financial planning, and ensuring compliance with tax regulations. The state monitored revenue collection and addressed issues related to tax evasion and disputes.

2. Public Works and Infrastructure

- Infrastructure Development:
I. Urban Planning: The state was responsible for urban planning and the development of infrastructure, including roads, fortifications, and public buildings. This facilitated trade, defence, and administrative functions.

II. Irrigation and Agriculture: Investment in irrigation systems was crucial for enhancing agricultural productivity. The state funded and managed irrigation projects to support agriculture and ensure food security.

Maintenance and Upkeep:

I. Public Maintenance: The state managed the maintenance and upkeep of public infrastructure, including roads, bridges, and buildings. This was essential for ensuring the functionality and longevity of infrastructure.

3. Economic Regulation and Control

- Market Regulation:

I. Price Control: The state sometimes intervened in market pricing to prevent exploitation and ensure fair prices for essential goods. This included regulating maximum prices and managing market stability.

II. Quality Control: The state enforced standards for the quality of goods and services to ensure fairness and prevent fraud.

- Trade Regulation:

I. Trade Policies: The state regulated trade practices, including setting customs duties, managing trade routes, and overseeing market transactions. This helped in controlling economic activity and maintaining trade relationships.

II. Monopoly and Competition: Measures were taken to prevent monopolistic practices and promote competition, ensuring a balanced and efficient market.

4. Welfare and Social Support

- Public Welfare:

I. Relief Programs: The state implemented relief programs during times of crisis, such as famines or natural disasters. This included distributing essential goods and providing support to affected populations.

II. Charitable Activities: Support for the poor and vulnerable segments of society was part of state responsibilities. This included funding for public services, healthcare, and education.

- Social Infrastructure:

I.   Educational Institutions: The state supported the establishment of educational institutions and centers of learning. This contributed to intellectual development and skill building.

II. Healthcare Facilities: Investment in healthcare facilities and medical services was part of the state's role in promoting public health and wellbeing.

5. Economic Planning and Policy

- Strategic Planning:

I.   Economic Policies: The state developed and implemented economic policies to guide economic activities, manage resources, and promote growth. This included policies related to taxation, trade, and public investment.

II. Resource Management: Strategic planning involved managing natural and human resources effectively to support economic development and stability.

- Budgeting and Allocation:

I.   Financial Planning: The state engaged in financial planning to allocate resources for various functions, including administration, defence, and public welfare.

II. Budget Management: Effective budgeting ensured that resources were used efficiently and that financial needs were met without compromising economic stability.

6. Defence and Security

- Economic Impact:

I.   Defence Spending: Investment in defence and security was crucial for maintaining stability and protecting the state. This included funding for the military, fortifications, and security measures.

II. Economic Protection: Ensuring security and defence helped protect economic interests, trade routes, and resources from external threats and internal disturbances.

7. Legal and Administrative Functions

- Regulation of Economic Activity:

I. Legal Framework: The state established a legal framework to regulate economic activities, including property rights, contracts, and dispute resolution. This provided a basis for fair and orderly economic transactions.

II. Administrative Oversight: Effective administration involved overseeing economic activities, enforcing regulations, and ensuring compliance with laws and policies.

8. Economic and Cultural Patronage

- Support for Arts and Culture:

I. Cultural Investments: The state often supported arts and cultural activities, including the construction of temples, patronage of artists, and promotion of cultural practices. This contributed to the cultural and economic development of the region.

- Economic Legacy:

I. Historical Records: Ancient texts and records provide insights into the economic functions of the state, reflecting its role in managing resources, promoting development, and ensuring stability.

Conclusion: The economic functions of the state in ancient India encompassed a wide range of activities, including revenue collection, public works, economic regulation, welfare, and strategic planning. The state played a central role in managing resources, promoting economic stability, and supporting societal needs. Ancient texts like the Arthashastra provide valuable insights into the principles and practices guiding the state's economic functions, highlighting its importance in shaping economic and social outcomes in ancient Indian societies.

****